Swimming at Midnight

Also By John Matthias

POETRY

Bucyrus 1970

Turns 1975

Crossing 1979

Bathory & Lermontov 1980

Northern Summer 1984

A Gathering of Ways 1991

Beltane at Aphelion: Longer Poems 1995

TRANSLATIONS

Contemporary Swedish Poetry 1980
(with Göran Printz-Pahlson)

Jan Östergren: Rainmaker 1983
(with Göran Printz-Pahlson)

The Battle of Kosovo 1987
(with Vladeta Vucković)

EDITIONS

23 Modern British Poets 1971

Introducing David Jones 1980

David Jones: Man and Poet 1989

Selected Works of David Jones 1992

CRITICISM

Reading Old Friends 1992

Swimming at Midnight

Selected Shorter Poems

John Matthias

Swallow Press Ohio University Press

Athens

Ohio University Press, Athens, Ohio 45701
99 98 97 96 95   5 4 3 2 1
Swallow Press/Ohio University Press books are printed on acid-free paper ∞

Library of Congress Cataloging-in-Publication Data

Matthias, John, 1941-
    Swimming at midnight : selected shorter poems / John Matthias.
        p.   cm.
    ISBN 0-8040-0984-8 (cloth). —ISBN 0-8040-0985-6 (paper)
    1. Title.
    PS3563.A858S95   1995   95-1278
    811'.54—dc20   CIP

Swimming at Midnight is made possible in part by support from the Institute for
Scholarship in the Liberal Arts, College of Arts and Letters, University of Notre
Dame. The author also acknowledges support from the Ingram Merrill Founda-
tion for grants during the 1984 and 1990 academic years during which some of
the poems in this book were written.

For Diana, Cynouai, and Laura

Contents

III

IV

V

Foreword

This book replaces my new and selected poems of 1984, *Northern Summer*. Although it is about eighty pages shorter, it also includes poems written in the intervening decade. I have tried, however contradictory it may sound, both to reduce the length and expand the contents. The length has been reduced chiefly by eliminating cycles such as "Northern Summer" itself, the "Stefan Bathory" and "Mihail Lermontov" poems, and indeed any poem at all running to more than eight or nine pages. These now appear, together with my other longer poems, in a companion volume called *Beltane at Aphelion* published simultaneously with the present book by Swallow Press. *Swimming at Midnight* is essentially a book of selected shorter poems.

I take my title from the first poem in the book, which is also the earliest, having been written in California in 1963. "Swimming at Midnight" is a phrase that means something different to me now from what it did more than thirty years ago. What served as the title of a young man's poem about skinny dipping now suits all too well many of the poems at the end of this book. The last poem of all, for example, is also a kind of swimming at midnight.

I have not, on the whole, organized this book strictly chronologically or volume by volume, but rather in such a way that poems in close proximity to one another here might conduct a dialogue somewhat different from the one that took place in the books from which they are selected. This has meant, in particular, shuffling together in the first four sections groups of poems which are stylistically compatible or complementary that first appeared in *Turns, Crossing,* and the last section of *Northern Summer.* In doing this, however, I have maintained an approximate chronology with respect to several largely autobiographical poems. I am happy to restore to print some poems from *Turns* and *Crossing* that were excluded from *Northern Summer,* and to find a place for several pieces written long ago that have never before appeared in a book.

I should say a word about the British contexts, settings, and sources for many of these poems. This is an American book by an American poet, but I have, both through design and accident, spent much of my writing time in England. Throughout the 1970s and the first half of the following decade, I wrote exclusively in England. The East Anglian region, in particular, became important to me over the years, and many of the poems in this book deal with historical, geographical, topological, and cultural matters which I would probably never have cared or written about had I not lived for a long time both in Cambridge and in my wife's family home near the Aldeburgh coast in Suffolk. Place is important to these poems. Having been deeply changed as a person and a poet by living where I chanced to live, I can only hope that something of my feeling for the place is given back in the poems, and that it is made comprehensible to American readers.

With the exception of the John Rothenstein monologue, shorter poems written since the publication of *Northern Summer* appear in Part V. If they seem to be relatively few in number, that is because my main activity between 1985 and 1991 was the composition of the three long poems which became *A Gathering of Ways* and are now reprinted in *Beltane at Aphelion*. I have also printed in Part V the Octavio Paz fragments from *Turns*, thinking that they belong with the translations and derivations establishing a context for several poems dealing with religious and historical issues with points of origin in Kosovo, Bosnia, and Languedoc. Only one of these poems was written as a kind of commentary on the tragedy of the former Yugoslavia. That the others might seem to have been only suggests that one engages with such issues at the risk of entering the very storm one thought had blown itself into oblivion. "Bogomil in Languedoc," "The Singer of Tales," and "The Silence of Stones" were all written in or before 1989; "Public Poem" was written in 1990.

I have not wanted to clutter the text with dates of composition or first publication. (A very few poems have dates in their titles, and one, "Poem for Cynouai," dates its interrupted period of composition at the conclusion.) Should a chronologically-minded reader wish to notice, I have indicated in the table of contents the book from which each poem has been selected according to the following parenthetical shorthand:

(B) = *Bucyrus,* 1970
(T) = *Turns,* 1975
(C) = *Crossing,* 1979
(NS) = *Northern Summer,* 1984
(*) = Previously unpublished in book form

JOHN MATTHIAS

Acknowledgements

Acknowledgement is due to the following journals which first published the poems appearing here in book form for the first time: *PN Review, Image, Salmagundi, The New Criterion, Stand, TriQuarterly, Argo, The Translation Review.*

Swimming at Midnight

[*Near my grandparents' home at the outskirts of town, a stone quarry was established, then abandoned, nearly a hundred and fifty years ago. The early blasting hit water, and after many soundings were taken, the management concluded that they had uncovered a bottomless lake, fed, they surmised, by a sizeable underground river.*]

Under a pine and confusion:
ah! Tangles of clothes: (come
on, silly, nobody's here:) and
naked as fish, a boy and a girl.
(Nobody comes here: nobody looks:
nobody watches us watching us
watch.) Except the police.
Thighs slide into the moon.
Humbly, into the stars: Mirrored,
flashes a father's red eye, a
blue-bitten mother's red lip: No
Swimming Allowed In The Quarry
At Night. (Anyway, nevertheless
and moreover: feel how warm!) here,
among the reflections. (Feel the
water's mouth and its hands, feel
them imitate mine: can there truly
be any danger?) danger allowed in
the quarry at night? can people
really have drowned? (Now my body
is only water alive, and aeons
ago you were a fish growing
legs—) well, dust to dust, a
curious notion. But quarry water on
dust green with seed! Quarry water
forbidden on land after dark! What
young forms of vegetation emerge.
What new colors of light.

Fathers

I never knew them.
Neither one. That
ancient Englishman
was deaf and in-
accessible—I

took his daughter
from his house.
He was dreaming
of ships, of Vienna,
his German assassin

sleeping under
his bed:
I never knew.
In Republican
Ohio, the man

I thought I
hated grew so
thin he'd slip
he said a wedding
ring around his

upper arm. Rheumatic,
he rode like a horse
his electrical in-
valid chair.
He was a judge

and should have
been a sailor . . .
Who'd stand no
nonsense, tell
them of the Empire

and by God Britannia,
chew his pipe
and try to
understand his girl—
twenty-one and

born when
he was fifty.
And if I'd known them,
either one, if I'm a
sailor now and should

have been a judge,
what son will talk
to me? What stranger
take my daughter from
a daughter's house?

Survivors

I

A letter arrives in answer
To mine—but six years late . . .
"John," it says,
                    "Dear John . . ." and
"I remember absolutely nothing.
What you say is probably
All true; for me those
Years are blank. I believe
You when you say you knew
Me then, that we were friends,
And yet I don't remember you
At all, or all those others
Who had names, or anyone. You see,

The fittest don't survive—
It's the survivors."

II

Like old women, burying their
Husbands, burying their sons, lasting
It out for years without their breasts
Or wombs, with ancient eyes,
Arthritic hands, and memories like
Gorgeous ships they launch
Despairingly to bring back all
Their dead, and which, as if constructed
By some clumsy sonneteer, betray them
Instantly and sink without a trace.

III

Or women not so old—
                    but always
Women, not the men who knock
Their brains and bodies against
Fatal obstacles & spit their blood
On pillows & their hearts on sleeves
At forty-five to die of being fit.

I've known a woman keep her watch
Beside a bed of botched ambition
Where her man lay down & took
Five years to die . . .

And though I drove one January night
Through freezing rain into Ohio—
And though I hurried,
Seeking the words of the dying—
All I found was a turning circle of women,
All I heard was the lamentation of survivors.

Rhododendron

Several years ago, you planted
near my study window something green.
Today I notice it, not just green,

but blazing red-in-green exactly
like the rhododendron it turned out
to be when you said: *Look!*

My rhododendron's flowering.
As usual, I had never asked, had
never noticed, would not have

had an answer if our daughter or
her friend had said a day ago: *And that?*
Just what is that? It's something green,

I'd have had to say, *that your mother*
planted there, some kind of flower
that hasn't flowered yet, although

she planted it three years ago.
It's the word itself, I think, that's
made it flower, and your saying it.

The winter's not been easy, and the
spring's been slow. I stared at long white
papers full of emptiness and loss

as one might stare at rows of narrow
gardens full of snow. The words
have not come easily, have not come well.

Easily you tell me, stepping through
the door: *Look! my rhododendron's*
flowering. . . . And it is, and it does.

In Columbus, Ohio

Cautiously, hoping that nobody sees,
    I stop my hired car outside your house.
You are not there, but far away
    in California putting your children to bed—
Nor have I seen you once in fifteen years.
    It's past eleven: your mother's floating by
A window in a purple robe, your father's
    reading a book. They have both been sick.
Like all their friends, they've had their
    operations, retired from their jobs, and begun,
To their annoyance, talking—like any poet—
    of the past.

What if we had married? The notion seems
    outrageously absurd, and yet, before our lives
Began in earnest, that, as I recall, was once
    indeed the plan. For years, I preferred your
House to mine, your parents to my own. . . .
    And then I loathed them, thought these shadows
At the window pane were guilty of offences
    intellectual and moral, that they drove you
Crazy to extremes of anarchy and lust through
    their chaste example & their discipline when
All the virginal austerity was mine.

What I want to do, you see, is to leap from
    the car, pound on the door, and say:
Forgive me! as they stand there staring in the
    autumn night. . . . (Perhaps we'd spend
An hour drinking brandy then, and tell long tales,
    and show each other photographs,
And shake hands solemnly at twelve. . . .) But
    of course I don't do anything like
That at all. I start the car and drive on East
    as far as Philadelphia.

U.S.I.S. Lecturer

— Amsterdam, Kalverstraat, March

What I hear at first is *Heren* and then *Heroine.*
Then the sudden toothy Dutchman
Ages dreadfully and vaguely threatens
Something, turns American,
And says with perfect clarity: "Heroin,

Like *smack.*" We stare each other down.
Eyes gone, muscles gone, he is teeth & yellow paper.
Still, I sense he is about my age.
I brush on past him, mind all wheeling
Backwards out of gear

To 1961 when I was here before and just eighteen.
What I dreamed into the streets of Amsterdam
Was Love: pure, high, unyielding,
Disdainful, and serene.
An appallingly beautiful bawd said she'd

Take my friend and me together. He
Went in alone, and for a moment I could see
Them swimming in the gaudy lights
Behind her fishbowl window. Someone opened up
A paper and I read: *Hemingway Zelfmoord.*

A decade and a half. I'm here to lecture twice
On a man who was my teacher once
Who, that very afternoon, in hot America,
Sat down aching and wrote out:
"My mother has your shotgun." And:

"It's so I broke down here."
In the middle of his poem, he meant.
I heard myself quote Woody Allen to a group
Of students yesterday in Leiden when
They asked me what I thought they could believe in.

Sex and death, I said.
Part of me's gone rotten as my junkie-brother's eyes.
Respectful and respectable, I took
A check from my ambassador
And quoted Woody Allen's quip to get a laugh.

I forgot to say: "*It was as he wrote his poem,*
You understand. His father
Had self-murdered too." Somewhere there,
In 1961 or so, was Love.
I'll think about the man who wrote the poem.

Edward

Edward, Edward, how we fear the sick!
I think I can almost remember you
whose name I'm called, John Edward.
Your illness was a terror
for us all. We, your nephews, marvelled
in our fear. We didn't know
exactly what the sick know, but we
knew they know—O things forbidden to the fit.
You were a kind of Shaman for us then.

We watched you jerk from chair
to cane, we watched you jam your gears, repeat,
walk backwards through the door,
then freeze and point, all man of ice,
at something moving after it had moved,
and then unfreeze, unlock,
and then repeat: *I do it then, I do it then.*

You gave us candies made of malted milk
and the family left you dying
in your corner chair. You had the post-war
sleeping-sickness, and you mostly slept:
through our lives, through your own.
There seemed no pity for you in that house.
For me, it was a magic time. I loved
my cousin then the way a boy of eight can
love a boy of ten. What could any of us do
for you? We took your candy and we fled.

Everybody fled: to their lunches or their jobs,
to their games or their affairs.
The other, boozy uncle said: *He was an ass-man once.*
For days I wondered what he meant.
Edward, did you curse us all the way you
might have, Shaman-like and darkly, silently:

So go off to your God-damned job and leave me here.
Your lunch. Your girl. Kid, go ride your bike
into a fucking truck. Who knows what you thought.
The children fled with the adults.

But when your brother in his final illness wept,
and when I had no pity, when I couldn't
stand to hear him say like any eight-year-old:
You made me cry, and when he said just audibly
enough for me to hear: *Go back to your*
God-damned books, then, Edward, I thought
I could remember you almost
and me a book-man, not an ass-man, now.
Edward, Edward, how we fear the sick!
Such counsels O
they give us of mortality.

If Not a Technical Song American:
Statement, Harangue, and Narrative

I Statement

Just last night I read your poems to the President.
You don't believe me, but I really did.
He broke down completely and
Wept all over his desk.
Now that I've done my work, you can relax.
Everything's going to be o.k.

And I read your poems to a joint session of Congress.
I read your poems to the FBI and the CIA.
Now that I've done my work, you can relax.
Everything's going to be o.k.

II Harangue

Your tired evasions, euphemism-lies.
Civilized man and his word-hoard.
Will you be relinquant
Or relinquished.

Name and Title. Religion and Rank.
Put a check in the column.
Put a check in the bank.

If you'd be only a little bit clever.
If you'd be occasionally.
If you'd be forever.

If you'd be my government.
If you'd be my gal.
If you'd be my treason and my tongue.

If anything articulate remains,
Identify the numbers by the names.

III Narrative

Cachectic, cachectic.
Heart rate grossly irregular.
Jugular venous distention.
Systolic expansile pulse.

Right ventricular lift.
Left ventricular tap.
Murmur along the sternal borders.
Pulmonary edema.

All piezometers installed
In the boreholes.
Static and dynamic
Cone penetration made.

Infra-red results
Allow mathematical models.
I hope I was never
Complacent: Seismology.

BUT IF I WAS IN LOVE WITH YOU?
I was in love with you, I think.
I think I didn't have the heart.

No, I never even thought to move the earth.

Diptych

I

Carpet flames.
Chain grip: incense
in a cup. Violins
and mandolins re-
corded. Oddly off.
Stumble dancer,
rafter slanting down.
(What is now beyond
you now my dear?)
Hold it (having
hardened) with a kiss.
He had lied
for years.

II

Zero on ice.
Tire spun: smoke
to three A.M. Hail
and also headlight
dimming. Oddly out.
Weep then weeper,
headlight out and hail.
(Who is now beside
me now and dear?)
Break it (having
buckled) with a fist.
She had cried
for years.

For John, After His Visit: Suffolk, Fall

Soldati's band shook Patty Fenelon's house
    last Spring so badly that the
Bookcase toppled down and spilled the cheap
    red wine on three authentic South
Bend, Indiana drunks. . . .
                For you, who love
    the elegiac and, if you believed
The arts you practice had in fact a chance
    of life at all, would prophesy
A new Romantic muse for all of us, how
    can I speak generously enough
About the life we've shared—the rich neurotic
    squalor of the midwest's Catholic
Mecca (. . . you a convert, me a Roman guest—
    cloistered there together preaching
Culture to the grandsons of Italian immigrants,
    the sons of Irishmen and Poles)?

You must, you always told me,
    have intensity. Half your students
Always thought you mad. Like Gordon
    Liddy on a job you'd go
To them bewigged and bearded bearing with
    you some incongruous foreign
Object—a Henry James harpoon or a Melvillian
    top hat—while through the hidden
Speakers blared your tape of Colin Davis and
    the BBC crooning Elgar on the
Last night of the Proms. Light in darkness, John!
    And all your manic gestures were serene.

Yeats to Lady Gregory, Nineteen Hundred & Four:
    "I did not succeed at Notre Dame."
He began to think his notions seemed "the thunder
    of a battle in some other star"; the thought
Confused him and he lectured badly; later he
    told tales with the "merry priests".

So you were not the first to feel estranged! And
         oh the thunder of your battle in that
Other star, its foolishness and grace. Beyond that
         fiddle, though, intensity was real
Enough for both of us.

How was I to know, returning from the dusty
         attic room where I had gone, where
I had often gone from midnight until three, and
         seeing you stare vacantly across
Your desk and through your lighted study
         window at the February snow that
You should truly be in love with my young
         friend, with that same lonely girl?

Was that the week you thought your son was ill?
         When you waited frightened while the
Severed head of Johnny's Siamese cat melted grinning
         in its package of dry ice padlocked in
The Greyhound baggage room in Indianapolis? The
         tests were negative, the bites
And scratches healed. . . .
                              Hiking on a treadmill
         at the clinic, I tested badly on a
Winter afternoon myself. I traded polysyllables
         with cardiologists who hooked me to their
Apparatus, checked my pressures, watched my blips
         on television screens, and asked me all
The secrets of my heart. . . .

Once we hiked together on the muddy banks of the
         St. Joseph, then across a farm. Your
Children ran ahead. They led you, while you
         talked in words they could not hear,
Haranguing me about the words you sometimes spoke
         when you would only speak, to credit
For a moment, because they looked at all around
         them, tree and bush and flower, because
They did not name and did not need to name, the
         eluctable modality of all you saw.

What more homely elegiacs, John, than this:
    reading backwards in a diary from
May—May to January, January twenty-fifth . . . and
    all my pulses skip. My father's gestures
Of exhausted resignation cease; he drops his cup
    of Ovaltine and stares into my
Mother's eyes amazed. . . . No dream, even, did he
    send me in my mourning time, no news
At all. . . . As a child I saw irregularities signaled
    in the pulsings of distended veins
Running up his temples and across his wrists:
    more affaires de coeur. . . .
                                    You made
Your trip among the dead ten years ago
    but found a Christian God along
The way in Barcelona. Did I take for politics
    your strange Falangist quips
The day we met?

December last, a month before my father's death,
    a quiet Christmas eve with sentimental
And nostalgic talk, some carolling. . . . Suddenly
    the blood. Stalking through a dark
And quiet house with automatic rifle and grenades
    you'd kick a bedroom door to bits and
Blast the sleeping couple in their bed, sprinkling
    holy water everywhere—your own obsessive
Dream. "I must have savagery," a wealthy British
    poet told me, leaving for the States.
I've gone the other way. My next door neighbor
    pounded at my door on Christmas eve; his
Bleeding wounds were real. What was all of England
    to a single one of his desires? When
I needed help you harbored me.

I wonder if our quarrel touches writing desks,
    like Mandelstam's with Pasternak. The
Greater man required none, the other poet did.
    Behind each artifact of any worth,
Cocteau insists, there is a house, a lamp, a fire,
    a plate of soup, a rack of pipes,

And wine. The bourgeoisie as bedrock. Mandelstam
     would crouch in corners listening to
The burning in his brain. If you're a Russian
     Jew because I am a wanton I am Catholic.

So what's the Devil's wage? Your riddling military
     metaphors unwind from Clausewitz and you
Will not say; your Faust, de Sade in neat quotations
     will not do. In London monographs on
Mahler are delivered in the morning post intended
     for the eyes of diplomats on holiday in
Devon—the still & deadly music of the IRA. One
     by one these books explode . . . In the hands
Of an unlucky clerk, the lap of an astonished secretary
     dreaming of her lover.

Stranger, then, and brother! John, these last three
     nights I've listened for you here,
Listened for you here where off the North Sea
     early Autumn winds bring down the
Twigs and bang the shutters of this house
     you came to bringing with you
Secrets and your difficult soul. In disintegrating
     space we are an architecture of sounds.
And you are not returning.

On a Slip of the Tongue

". . . and in my father's life at the very end of his mind . . ."
Imogen Holst, BBC 3

And what *was* in
your father's life

At the very end
of his mind?

A sound, a sound
was in his mind

At the very end
of his life

But what was found
in his life & wound

At the very end
of his mind?

Once for English Music

I

This, this is marvelous,
   this is simply too good—
I am their song, Jeremiah!
   Elgar on The Folk.

And I have worked for forty years
   and Providence denies
Me hearing of my work. So I submit:
   God is against it,

Against art. And I have worked
   for forty years and
Providence denies. And Strauss (R.),
   1905: I drink

To the welfare of the first
   English progressive.
And Gerontius: pray for me, my friends,
   who have no strength to pray.

II

And who would not put out—with his mother
Or his Queen—the night light,

Toothbrush, bathrobe and condom,
Run the bath, switch on the stereo,

Plug in the fire, and wait for time
To reverse, wait for a Prince to rise

From the dead & conduct his affairs?
Neither you nor I, neither mine nor yours.

III

There in the James Gunn portrait,
There, almost, in the Beecham life—

Delius who wasn't really English,
Delius who got around:

Dying, did he summon in his cripple's dream
A syphilitic and promiscuous librettist

(In a summer garden, or on hearing the
First cuckoo in Spring)?

He would compose.
He would have his way with words.

IV

During the performance
    of an overture, said Shaw,
By one of the minor Bachs,
    I was annoyed
By what I took to be the jingling
    of a bell-wire somewhere.
But it was Dr Parry. Playing the
    cembalo part . . . on a
Decrepit harpsichord.

V

Fluctuating sevenths,
    fluctuating thirds.
I'll play it on my flute
    the way it sounds.

In Surrey, in Sussex,
    airs against the harmon-
Izing organist from
    Worthing. . . .

For Why Do The Roses?
   Because we sing enchanted.
Because we chant
   And sing.

Three Around a Revolution

I A Gift

He is the Tribune of The People,
He is Babeuf. The others speculate,

But he is Babeuf. The others
Speculate and steal. Gracchus

Out of Plutarch, he takes
The crudely fashioned knife

Made by his son from a candlestick
For his (the father's) suicide.

He hones it on his eloquent tongue.
He says, smiling enigmatically:

Here, it is yours. Do what you can.

II Alternatives

One announces in papers:
Seeking the patronage of the rich

To further my work. For a decade
It will always be noon.

Nobody's wealth intervenes
Between freedom and time.

One in despair discharges a gun:
Nevertheless, he goes on writing

Noblesse oblige with seven balls
Of shot in his brain.

Making accurate measurements,
Another says: Here we may build,

Here we may bathe, here we may breathe.

III   A Letter

There must be horses, there must be women,
There must be lawsuits. There must, moreover

And eventually, be justice. There must be words.
I write down words. Are we lost in our names?

Yesterday I spoke for hours and nobody stirred.
Rapt. They cheered. I am a hero.

I said words like *action, money, love, rights*
And was moved to elegance, alliteration,

Saying, apropos of what I did not know,
Palfrey, palindrome, pailing, palinode, palisade.

Bakunin in Italy

Wagner's face is still illuminated
Over Dresden in that fire I fed

And in the glow of it I see my sister
Walking through the snow beside Turgenev.

Did I spit my teeth out in the Peter-Paul
Only to release the homicidal genius

Of Nachaev? I should have been a Jesuit,
A Mason. Castrati sing the Internationale

And dance the choreography of Karl Marx.
I should have been a tenor playing

Sophie Hatzfeldt in an *opéra bouffe*
By Ferdinand Lassalle.

Alexander Kerensky at Stanford

He rose one Winter from his books
To sit among the young, unrecognized.

It was 1963. It was 1917.
He sipped his coffee & was quite anonymous.

Students sat around him at their union
Talking politics: Berkeley, Mississippi.

A sun-tanned blonde whose wealthy father
Gave her all his looks and half his money

Whispered to her sun-tanned lover:
"Where *is* Viet Nam?"

He thought no thought of theirs.
In his carrel at the Hoover Institute

He had the urns of all his ancient enemies.
Their dust was splattered on his purple tie.

E. P. in Crawfordsville

(for D. D. in South Bend lecturing on
"Enlightenment and Christian Dissent")

He was *en provence* for sure
at Wabash college—
Writing there to Mary Moore
of Trenton, "Grey eyes . . ."

Writing *Cino:* "Bah! I have
sung women in three
cities . . .", putting up an
unemployed actress,

getting fired, *Gay Cino*
of quick laughter,
Cino, of the dare, the jibe.
What, asked Possum more

than once, does Ezra Pound
believe? In light. In
light from the beginning,
in gardens of the sun—

But "'Pollo Phoibee, old
tin pan," in Crawfordsville?
Age des lumieres! Bold
Polnesi, Jefferson, Voltaire—

light inside the acorn-seed
on Zeus's aegis-day
when he'd become indeed
the lack-land Cino

having sung & sung the sun
for thirty years in
every kind of city, light
converging into one

great ball of crystal
silent as some Hoosier
Presbyterian at prayer
along the Wabash.

Six for Michael Anania

I   Trithemius

Orifiel reigned:
   March 15
      the first year of the world.

So, Trithemius, timid and wise.
So, Agrippa. Light!

Paid the debts at Sponheim.
Drove the lazy monks.
God's breath, good books: stone.

Vulgar speak of vulgar things.
So, Agrippa. Light!

Maximilian in my
   cunning circle
      trod.

II   Agrippa von Nettesheim

Nothing less than total reform
Mystical. Of the world.

Margaret of Austria, O Mirific Maid,

August, divine, and very clement chick,
I'm on the dole.

The Nobility of Women Folk—
Exalt I phrases here . . .
Dollars for the scholars, sweetheart; smile.

So that Franciscan calls me heretic.
So Inquisitor Savini burns his share.
Frogs' eyes. Mule piss.
Everyone's Pythagorean here.

III Paracelsus

All things change save one.
All things one save change.

Re-ligare means unite again.

Areopagite of Athens,
Follow *now*. Where?

The patients of the Galenians died.

And in her hand
  (the Queen's)
    I'll put a rose.
And in his hand
  (the King's)
    I'll put a golden crown.

And in the sea aboard their ship
The King he'll take his Queen.

The patients of the Galenians died.

IV Nostradamus

The curious words remain. The seer sees.
Single combat on a lawn; the bloody axe.

Out of time, he travels in it still.
Catherine de Medici knows. Henry II is warned.

The act occurs as it is seen the act occurred.

Out of time, he traveled in it still.
Catherine de Medici knew. Henry II was warned.

The curious words remained. The seer saw.
Single combat on a lawn; the bloody axe.

The act occurred as it is seen the act occurs.

V Rosencreutz to Saint-Germain

We did not mean Brother Martin.
We did not mean 30 Years War.

We did not mean Huguenots
Or St. Bartholomew's Eve.

We did not mean property.
We did not mean money.

We did not mean Pope
Or the Place de la Grève.

But no more maneuvers.
All are vowed to death.

Too late. I have done all I can.

VI

Qualities tend
To Perfection.

We may assist.

Double Sonnet on the Absence of Text: "Symphony Matis der Maler", Berlin, 1934:—Metamorphoses

I

The eschatology of Jews and Christian heretics:
Unearthly metal glows. *Schafft er nicht mehr—*
He lies among his tools.
Geh hin und bilde. Geh hin und bilde
Polyptich as polyphony. Medieval modes,
Matis: Gothardt, Neithardt. Grunewald
To historians, *der Maler.*
Father of no child though, Regina; father
Of his altarpiece at Isenheim, father
Of his torments, his tormentors,
Dying in obscurity at Halle building mills.
Geh hin und bilde. For Albricht, Luther
Or for Muntzer? *Geh hin und bilde.*
The pointing finger of an evangelic hand
Outlasts apocalypse.

II

The libretto: that's the crux, the words.
Because of that the senile Strauss would
Play *Gebrauchsmusik* for Goebbels who, while
Furtwängler's applauded by the partisans
Of Brecht or Grosz or Benn, sits
On hams beside the corpse of Wagner.
Oh that Hindemith should feel the pull
Of Matis: What's the distance, then, from
Buchenwald to Yale? *Ist, dass du*
Schaffst und bildest, genug?
Abandoned, all the words: for what
They cannot settle will be left alone.
Leaving us just where, Professor?
Contemplating cosmogonic harmonies with Kepler.
In oblivion with courage and acoustics.

On the Death of Benjamin Britten

Operas! A feast for burghers, said Adorno.
And of your work: The apotheosis
Of meagerness, a kind of fast. That's
A cruel case against you
And it may have weight, in time.
But let's call meagerness
Economy today
And call the bourgeoisie the people
Who like me have (barely) what it costs
To listen and who like to hear
These songs, but who will pay a price.
Economies of living soon enough
Make meager even music of the spheres!
To be of use, you said.
Directly and deliberately I write
For human beings. And not
Posterity—for which the general outlook
Isn't very bright.

A tenor mourns. And you lie down in Aldeburgh
One last time. But you have work to do
In spite of what the two of us have said.
A tenor sings. When you
Get out there over the horizon
This December morning with the likes
Of Peter Grimes,
Row your shining boat ashore
And be extravagant in song:
Leave economy to the ungrateful living
Who will need it, whose Justice
And whose History have multiplied unendingly
Expenses by Apotheoses by Sublimes.

Brandon, Breckland: The Flint Knappers

(after a chapter in Julian Tennyson's *Suffolk Scene*)

The Forestry Commission was about to plant
the Breckland on the day young Julian Tennyson

visited the Edwardses, last knappers of Brandon.
Because some tribes in Central Africa

hadn't heard about percussion caps
there still was business for the craftsmen

that supplied the flint for Wellington
and watched the plovers & the curlews dip at home.

Alien, the Breckland seemed as sinister & desolate
to Tennyson as 1938, the stark flint cottages

all shining darkly in reflecting pools
of stone and dusty sorrel, riding in the ragwort

and the bugloss, or jutting out of bracken,
heather, thin brown grass.

Wheatears, stonechats, whinchats, pipits—
all in the same still air—

and Julian, once a Suffolk countryman's Huck Finn,
feeling terrors coming on him

now at twenty-three, feeling *loosed in some
primeval, flat and limitless arena*—

leagues and leagues and leagues of it, he wrote,
severed from the rest of England.

Brandon on the Little Ouse was a relief from that;
though still in Breckland.

Malting, watermeadows, fine old bridge—
as lovely a corner as any I have found in Suffolk.

The elder Edwards, coughing, takes him
in his workshop, shuts the door, and points:

topstone, wallstone, floorstone chips
from Lingheath Common quarry, ornaments & tinders,

flints for muskets, carbines, pistols—
quartered first, then flaked and knapped with

pointed hammer on a flattened rod of iron.
When the headmen learn about percussion caps

the show's all over, Edwards said.
And anyway we've not got one apprentice

and the quarrier's retired. It would die with him,
his art, these mysteries of Breckland.

Meanwhile Tennyson looks on amazed
as Edwards bevels edges, hammers, hammers, talks:

I did it on the radio into a microphone, I
did it on the BBC before the news.

There are reports. Off in Central Africa
sprawls a man who feels of a sudden loosed in some

primeval flat and limitless arena—
leagues and leagues and leagues of it, he thinks

in his delirium. There is a flight of birds.
On Berner's green: an Air Ministry bombing-ground;

here the Forestry Commission will plant firs.
Badgers and foxes, jays and crows

will populate the land the curlews flee, *and when*
the Old Guard fell before great Wellington

England sang the knappers of the Brandon flints!
It is the year of Munich. Tennyson will die

in Burma from a piece of shrapnel the size of any
smallish hag-stone he'd have found

among discarded chips on Edwards' dusty floor
and which his copy of George Borrow

pressing pages from a manuscript of *In Memoriam*
will not deflect. Reflected in his book,

an Indian summer. Ice will one day lift
the Blaxhall Stone itself as far as Brandon moor.

59 Lines Assembled Quickly
Sitting on a Wall Near the Reconstruction
of the Lady Juliana's Cell

Heavily   heavily
hidden away—

the door is
barred & barred   and

singing
veni creator

spiritus "a service
of Enclosure"

& the cell
is consecrated

and the door
is barred   and

singing
veni creator

spiritus you have
a window on

the church you have
a window on

the world
and appearances

and revel-
ations   visions!

"showings"
to a soul *that*

cowde
no letter: cowde—

could, cloud
no cloud or cold

unknowing sin
is what

there loud? or
quiet sin is what

behoved? or is
behovable

il convient que
le péché

existe: le péché is
serviceable

what is
an anchorhold what is

an anchoress
the Lady Juliana's

one re-
corded visit from the

frenzied Margerie Kempe
as praise

& praise & gesture
I prefer

to Juliana's
Kemp's

the *other* Kemp's
Will Kemp's

who Morris-danced
from London

days   on days
from London

Kemp's who
lept!   immortally

this Norwich wall

26 June 1381/1977

I North Walsham: The Fields

And he, Despenser, tried to keep hold
Of the dyer's head

As the crowd of them, gawkers
& priests, tinkers & tailors & wastrels

(Gentry too, thinking already: *reredos!*
A gift for him, a

Presentiment) lurched along
With the horsecart off to the place

Of undoing, Lidster's undoing who'd heard—
Who'd heard of *The Kynges*

Son who'd paye for al,
The mullere who'd ygrounde smal—but

Was paying himself,
Tied by a foot with the same rope

That they'd hang him with, after
The drawing. And he

Henry Despenser, the Bishop "Lespenser"—
miles amatus, boni pastoris mens,

For so it says on his brass—
Hopping behind the cart like a toad,

The cart they dragged the dyer behind
For that was the law:

To be dragged to the place of undoing.
This, however, was extra:

The Bishop himself coddling your head
In his skirts

And you "The King of the Commons",
"The Idol of Norfolk"

Whose bell had been rung
By Ball and Tyler and Straw. Oh

This dispenser of justice was special,
sui generis the man who

Had caught you, tried you, confessed you,
The man who would hang you

See you in quarters, one for each of
The earth's: hopping

Behind the cart like a toad . . .
And reaching out for your head   which

Aoi!   he'd drop on a cobble a cobble
a cobble and *there*

Then catch it up again, mother it back
In his apron, your head

Like an apple or melon or globe. Where,
Where did you travel, where

Did you think you could go—
The two of you, then, staff, of one, life?

II   St Luke's Chapel, Norwich Cathedral

We look at the reredos, the retables.
Of course the "subject"

Is "Christ". . . . But the blood & the power
That steadied the hand

And shook the knees and the wits of the
Master from Norwich—*that*

Was the blood and the power of Dyer
And Bishop, of Lidster

And Henry Despenser. Behind me somebody
Mumbles the word *chiliastic.*

His fellow-tourist says, looking hard: it's
Absolutely fantastic!

The five panels escaped the smashings
Of Cromwell. The five

Scenes from the Passion here are restored.
And we may embrace

The arcana, study
The photomicrographic specifics:

A patient lady explains: *malachite,*
Azurite: And the head of Christ is restored!

The rotten wood is restored: the order
Is restored. *Israelite,*

Trotskyite. Edmund Burke said of the famous
Rhyme: *it rhymes!* And also: *a sapient*

Maxim: When Adam delved and Eve span, who
Was then the gentle man?

Nobody knows what Lidster said, but that's
What he heard: *The Kynges son schal*

Paye for al
The mullere hath ygrounde smal—and

Paid it himself,
Tied by a foot with the same rope

They'd etcetera. *Spin:*
The painting and the restoration

Are brilliantly done. *Delve:* the revolt
Alas was untimely—even Engels

Would say so—and Henry Despenser's work
Was brilliantly done—

And us with our heads still on our necks?
With books in our laps,

Stupid or giddy, gawking—
Us with the eyes still in their sockets

And tongues still in our mouths—
Where do we travel, where

Do we think we can go—
All of us, now, staff, of one, life?

Turns: Toward a Provisional Aesthetic
and a Discipline

I

The scolemayster levande was the toun
and sary of hit semed everuch one.
The smal quyt cart that covert was and hors . . .
to ferien his godes. To ferien his godes
quere he was boun.

The onelych thyng of combraunce (combraunce)
was the symphonye
(saf a pakke of bokes)
that he hade boghte the yere
quen he bithoght
that he wolde lerne to play.

But the zele woned (zele woned).
He neuer couthe ani scylle.

II

And so the equivalent
          (the satisfactory text.
squ'elles sont belles
          sont pas fidèles. rough
west-midland, hwilum andgit
of andgiete: the rest is not
          a word for word defense. . . .

III

And make him known to 14th-century men
Even when everything favors the living?
Even if we could reverse that here
I know you've read and traveled too.

So Destination or Destiny: *Quere He Was Boun!*
And yet to introduce the antecedent place.
Restrictive clause; sense of the referent noun.
A tilted cart is a cart with an awning.

    Langland has it "keured"
    John of Mandeville "coured"
    Wycliffe "keuered"

    But "covert" in Arimathaea

Personal luggage: not the same as merchandise.
Cursor Mundi's "gudes"; Purity's "godes"

This is personal luggage / destination / travel

    Harp and pipe and symphonye

    (saf a pakke of bokes)

IV

Where dwelle ye if it tell to be?

    at the edge
        of the toun?
    at the edge
        of the toun?

Levande was.
He Levande Was The Toun.

Reason the nature of place
Reason he can praise
Reason what the good-doing doctor said

    Rx.:cart (that covert was & hors)

Dull ache in the hip is probably gout.
Painful nodes of calcium—(neck & in the ears).
Palpitations, flutters. Stones in the gland.

food to avoid?   drink

(put him in the cart)

Rx.:bibliography
Rx.:map

V

The metaphysicality of Hermetic thought—
Let him think o' that! (Problem is he
Still enjoys cunt . . .)

. . . instrument was ay thereafter
Al his own combraunce . . .

Sary of hit semed everuch one.

Torn between disgust & hope
He simply never couthe . . .

antiquorum aegyptiorum
oh, ... imitatus . . .

VI

All day long it rains. He travels
All day long. Wiping water from
His eyes: and twenty miles? and
Twenty miles? Fydlers nod & smile.

Cycles pass him. Cars pass him.
Buses full of tourists . . .
Dauncers & Minstrels, Drunkards
And Theeves. Whooremaisters,
Tossepottes; Maskers, Fencers
And Rogues; Cutpurses, Blasphemers
Counterfaite Egyptions . . .

Greek, Arabic, Medieval Latin,
Mis-translated, misconceived.
More than just for his disport

who loveth daliaunce

who falleth   (o who falleth)

far behinde . . .

VII

That supernatural science,
That rare art should seem . . .

here among
a randy
black-billed

ilk

Les traductions sont comme les femmes. And time to get off of her toes. Idiomatic: toes. Lorsqu'elles sont belles. I should apologize, then: to apologize. The schoolmaster was leaving the village, and everybody seemed sorry. Simple as that. The miller lent him the cart and horse to carry his goods. Simple as that. And no particular trouble with the words. Scolemayster: 1225 in the *Life of St. Katherine.* But you change the spelling, see, to conform with the dialect. Levande was: *The Destruction of Troy,* "all the Troiens lefton". But use the participial construction. Sary of hit: see the *Lay Folks Mass Book.* The city of his destination. Twenty miles off. Quite sufficient size for his effects. The only cumbersome article (save the pack of books) was: count on the medieval mind to be sympathetic. Though I come after hym with hawebake/I speke in prose and lat hym rymes make. My general principles I take from the King (and his Queen). Tha boc wendan on Englisc. Hwilum word be word. Hwilum andgit of andgiete. Swa swa ic hie geliornode. It would be idle and boring to rehearse. Here what is available. Let me simply indicate the manner. Take sulphur from Sol for the fire and with it roast Luna. From which will the word issue forth . . . *If* the given appeared in a verifiable text. *If* the given was truly equivalent.

The usual procedures are the following: (1) To ignore altogether: "make no effort to explain the fundamentals". (2) To drop apologetic footnotes: "I'm sorry, but I simply cannot understand this esoteric sort of thing". (3) To make suggestive remarks while hurrying on to something else: "*If* the given appeared in a verifiable text. *If* the given was truly equivalent". But the schoolmaster was leaving the village, and everybody seemed sorry. *Jude the*

Obscure, paragraph one, a neat linguistic exercise. Written by Thomas Hardy in 1895. And such a revelation makes the art available to the vulgar. Who will abuse and discredit? *Keeper of secret wisdom, agent of revelation, vision, and desire:* THIS IS THE QUESTION WE MUST ALWAYS RAISE.

Now some of the obscure, like some of the lucid, do not become proletarianized. Unlike the majority of their kind, they are not cast down from the ruling class to produce a commodity which both enslaves them and enslaves the exploited labourers with whom they are objectively allied. Perhaps they hold teaching jobs in public schools or universities; perhaps they have an inherited income. In any case, some maintain their Hermetic privilege. They are not obliged to live by their art or to produce for the open market. Such unproletarianized obscure are revolted by the demands of a commercialized market, by the vulgarity of the mass-produced commodity supplied to meet it. And revulsion ultimately tells (1) on their sex life (2) on their health.

While a relationship of cause and effect is established between obscure and lucid organizations emerging from the division of labour and the consequent dialectical evolution of social reality, such becomes, we know, increasingly separated from the actual productive function of society, from sleep. This gives us pause. "The point is that the notion of invariancy inherent by definition to the concept of the series, if applied to all parameters, leads to a uniformity of configurations that eliminates the last traces of unpredictability, of surprise." This gives us pause.

And so the system and its adherents are the villains; license, conspiracy, and nihilism are the virtues of the heroes: *or:* The system itself becomes a context for heroics; license, conspiracy, and nihilism become the crimes of the villains; acceptance of convention and austere self-discipline become the virtues of the heroes. The schoolmaster is forever an intermediary: the shape of his life is determined by the nature of society: the nature of his art seeks to determine the shape of society by administering to its nature. And intermediacy ultimately tells (1) on his sex life (2) on his health.

But make him known to 14th-century men even when everything favors the living. Reason the nature of place. Reason he can praise. Reason that he travels in a cart. With Cursor Mundi's "gudes"; with Purity's "godes". With Joseph of Arimathaea, turns: to elliptically gloss.

III

Spokesman to Bailiff, 1349: Plague

(". . . after which the bourgeoisie.")

We leave you payment.
In a cup of vinegar
Beside the well, the
Coins that you require.

Let no one approach us.
Here we make an end
Of ceremony, custom. In
Our wreckage all of

Europe's racked, your
Kindness unrequited in
Its kind. And yet our death's
A birth of avarice and

Powers oblique, unfathomed.
Leave us bread & ointments.
Free from obligations, we
Leave the world to its wealth.

Two Ladies

I

So many incorrupt bodies, such
Corrupting times!
Edmund to and fro for years,

Inspected, found intact,
Unburied & unbothered & unblemished
And then, then these ladies

These incorruptible ladies
Like Etheldreda Queen & Sainted Audrey
Earlier than Edmund even

Wearing round her neck a fabled string
Of beads that purpled flesh
Into a fatal tumor that she liked:

She had, she said, been vain.
Daughter of the hypothetical incumbent
Of the ship at Sutton Hoo,

Daughter of the priest who taught her,
Touchy and untouched—
By Tondbert Prince of Fenmen and

By Ecgfrith son of Osway the Northumbrian—
She ruled, queened, twice,
And got sick of it, of royalty, and fled:

Fled to Abbess Eba, solicitous and grave,
Where randy Ecgfrith followed
With his louts who'd leered at her around

The smutty fire inside the great log hall.
Flowering near Ely
Among fowlers, among fishermen & fogs—& bogs—

Famously her pilgrim's staff took root
& that was Etheldreda's Stow.
They say in Etheldreda's Stow today, they *say*—

That water bubbling from her temporary grave
Was Audrey's Spring: & any bauble
There that's worn around the neck's called tawdry.

II

Margery Kempe from Lynn
Would howl and wail "full plenteously"
When told of mirth & pleasures

"Full boisterously" she sobbed
Who was no Wycliffite or Lollard but
Could censure equally

Some bumpkin local reprobate or mighty
Philip Repington and
Greater Arundel upon his Bishop's throne.

Full plenteously, full boisterously
She'd wail: full homely, too!
She was her own Salvation Army band

And drummed and trumpeted vulgarity that
Such as Chesterton would
Understand to be an efficacious pastorale.

Some amanuensis took it down, our first
Biography—be glad! *She* was:
Of plenteous continual weeping by a creature

Who would be the bride of Christ, a pilgrim pure
And not the failed brewer, failed
Miller married to the borough chamberlain

John Kempe that she, said citizens of Lynn,
Pretty clearly was. Contentious;
Weird; she sailed away. The Mamelukes

And Saracens were less impressed with her
Outside the Holy Sepulchre
Than those who'd suffered her for weeks

On board the ship. Said one: a vexèd spirit.
Another: that she'd surfeited on wine.
A third that surely fatal illnesses came on

Like that: *O put her in a heavy sea*
O put her in a little boat
Without a bottom O. Thus, Amanuensis says,

Had each his thoughts. At
York, at Cawood Palace, the Archbishop:
"Woman!—Why, why

Then weepest thou?" And Margery: *Sir, ye*
Shall wish some day
That ye had wept as sore as I!

Words for Sir Thomas Browne

I

If melancholy is a sadness with no reasonable cause,
your son Tom's death at sea produced in you a grief

and not a melancholy. You would define, define again,
whose testimony helped convict, in 1655,

two witches in the court of Matthew Hale. Gentle man,
they hung on Suffolk gallows till they died.

You bore no kind of malice towards them, either one,
and you studied to avoid all controversy always.

But if no witches did the Devil's work, it followed
that no works were done among us by the Spirits,

and from that, no doubt "obliquely", that the hierarchy
of creation would collapse & neither New Philosophy

nor love could save the soul of your young Tom
who read & praised the pagans on his ship *whose noble*

straynes, you thought, *may well affect a generous mind.*
Amazed at *those audacities, which durst be nothing,*

and return into their Chaos once again, you recommended
orthodoxy and you testified for Matthew Hale.

II

Death was occupation and preoccupation both in Norwich
where you practiced medicine, exploded vulgar errors,

contemplated cinerary urns. You did not *secretly implore
& wish for plagues, rejoyce at famines,* or *revolve*

ephemerides in expectation of malignant aspects & eclipses
like certain others of your trade. Your prayers

went with the husbandmans, desiring *everything in proper*
season, that neither men nor times be out of temper.

But they were deeply & profoundly out of temper, the men
and times in your extraordinary time. New Science

studied to discern the cause and was itself part cause
and part effect. Love got on with its peculiar,

frail, sublunary affairs: and though you'd be *content that*
we might procreate like trees without conjunction,

husbands awkwardly attended to their husbandry, and you
yourself begot a dozen saplings. Of the seven who survived,

Edward was the firstborn and the doctor, but Tom was your
particular delight—& like to make, you thought, at once

a navigator & a scholar on that ship of Captain Brookes—
and like to take the draughts of all things strange.

III

Pythagoras and Lucan, Epicurus too: he took the draughts
of these and dwelt on noble suicides, on transmigrations,

and on souls that dwelt in circuits of the moon or souls
eternally annihilated in eternal night.

Audacious draughts: they'd make a generous mind so drunk
it might conceive itself invaded by the speech of Vulteius

and urge, in some engagement where a Netherlandish Pompey
stole the victory & then prevented honorable escape,

the sober Roman medicine you feared. How did Thomas die?
If he fell upon his sword, or, lost to Admiral Kempthorne,

lit a powder keg and blew his ship to kingdom come,
we never heard. If some malefic doctor set about to loose

a plague, or grinning crones beside a rocky coast at dawn
spun almanacks and made a storm, you never said.

You did your work: you sought to cure the ill & comforted
the dying, you strangled mice and chickens on your

kitchen scales to see if *weight increaseth when the vital
spirits flee,* you demonstrated that the elephant

indeed has joints, that beavers do not ever *in extremity
bite off their stones,* that no bear brings her

young into the world *informus and unshapen* to fashion them
by licking with her tongue, that Eve & Adam had no navels

and that Jesus wore (a Nazerite by birth) short hair.
Often you returned to your initial, fundamental ground:

Whatever impulse be unlocked by Lucan's strains, whatever
operation be insinuated in us when, Satanic,

we're inhabited by arguments which say *necessity* or *chance*
or *fate,* a lucid sense of order could, you thought,

when mixed in some alembic with humility & grace, explain
and purge away (though witches must, alas, be hanged).

IV

*As though the soul of one man passed into another,
opinions, after certain revolutions, do find men & minds*

like those that first begat them.

        Staring fixedly at Tom's
last letter in your hand, thinking of that trial where

one alleged his chimney had been cursed & yet another that
his cart had been bewitched and also all his geese,

you well might suddenly embrace that sweet & generous heresy
that tempted you when you were young: that all are saved—

yourself & Tom, those witches in the court of Matthew Hale,
Epicurus, Lucan & Pythagoras, cruel doctors who revolve

ephemerides, husbands who attend to husbandry, sons and
daughters, brothers aunts & sisters, wives.

And yet you said: *God saves whom he will* . . .
and thought the wretched women damned at Edmund's bury.

And thought you heard Tom's ship explode at sea.

You Measure John

for Diana, at work in the Fitzwilliam

For posterity you measure John.
For the catalogue
you measure with a tape
his works
and recognize yourself as woman
among women
in the life of this man John, his death.

You measure for the catalogue
the pictures
and their frames
thinking of the others
measuring his need
measuring his pride (who could not
please himself)
measuring his gypsy caravans of children
as he went away to paint, badly,
the famous and the rich.

No, you do not like Augustus John.
Measuring the thickness
of a new biography you offer me
I think—
not. You tell it simply
and with no embellishments yourself.
It is an old story:
some man damages the lives of women
who would love him.
There are various excuses.
One is art.

My Youngest Daughter: Running
Toward an English Village Church

Sunday, then. In Trumpington. And nearby bells.
My daughter runs among the village graves
this foggy January morning of her early youth
as I lie late in bed
and watch her from my window.

I know she holds her breath.
Superstitious, she'll hold it till she passes by
the final marker near the door & disappears inside.
If you breathe in cemeteries
you inhale evil spirits!
What do you inhale when you breathe in stony
churches or in bedrooms where you wake alone
and realize you cannot tell
your child's superstition from her faith?

Beyond the church, a village green, a meadow,
the pleasures and the picnics
of next spring. I tell her
not to hold her breath in graveyards.
Watching her red coat become a gaudy blur
against the brilliant hoarfrost,
I realize I'm holding mine.

Mark Twain in the Fens

I

Not the trip of 1872
when fame first fanned an Anglophilia
and glory burst from every side
upon him—
And not the trip of 1879
when he howled for *real coffee,
corn bread, good roast beef
with taste to it.*

The last trip; the exile & the debts.

*Thish-yer Smiley had a yeller
one-eyed cow that didn't have no tail.* . . .
At Brandon Creek, Ship Inn.
They bring him real coffee, good
roast beef with taste to it.

II

　　　　Recently got up
by him as Joan of Arc,
his eldest daughter once had fled
the Bryn Mawr auditorium—
meningitis all but creeping
up her spine—

He told them all a tingler,
having sworn to her he wouldn't,
called *The Golden Arm.*

　　　　Death made real by hers?
and deathless tales
a part of blame? *My fault, my fault—*
And this: *I'll pay*

though still he dreams each night
about his miracle-working
machine, the Paige Typesetter,
his Dark Angel of print.

III

Thish-yer Smiley had a yeller
one-eyed cow that didn't have no tail. . . .

No one writes it down
or sets it up in type. It is the last
he is going to tell.

It is all over with him. It's
begun. All night long
he tells and tells and tells.

Paul Verlaine in Lincolnshire

I

For a while he had that famous friendship.
But what's inspired debauchery
and manic vision
to illuminations from the English hymnal?
Keble's stanzas? Wesley's? Stanzas
by good Bishop Ken?
Ô mon Dieu, vous m'avez blessé d'amour.

For indulgence, there was Tennyson.
He walked to Boston from the grammar school
in Stickney to confess.

II

And wrote *Sagesse* there in Lincolnshire.
And went to chapel,
and taught the ugly boys finesse.
He had been condemned to death,
he boasted, in the Siege
of Paris . . .
        Colonel Grantham and
the credulous headmaster
listened to the story
of his clever rescue by Thiers. . . .

Even in the hands of Debussy, Fauré,
the Catholic *lied* Verlainian would sing
the strangest nonconformist airs.

Ô mon Dieu, vous m'avez blessé d'amour.

III

And to proper Mallarmé he wrote
about the absinthe: *I'd still take it
with sugar.* . . .
The school record books
do not suggest
that he excelled at rugger.

O there were many rhymes—
But he was on his best behavior,
pious, calm, bourgeois.
The peaceful English countryside
acted on his conscience
like a rudder.

Ô mon Dieu, vous m'avez blessé d'amour.

Friendship

One day I do you a good turn. Then
You do me *two* good turns.
I am pleased by that & say so the next day.

You break the lead in your pencil.
I loan you mine.
You give me an expensive fountain pen.

I play you a recording of The Modern Jazz Quartet.
Though you like Milt Jackson's vibes, you
Take me to *The Ring* at Covent Garden after which

We introduce each other to our wives.
My wife teaches your wife how to cook fondues.
Your wife teaches my wife how to live.

I dedicate my book to you & you are moved.
You make a character of me in yours:
It is singled out for praise by the reviewers.

I give my mistress to your loyalest disciple.
Claiming he is bored with her, you have
The wench returned; her skills are much improved.

When I sing my secret lute song about mountains,
You take me to the mountains
In your car: You have a cabin there

Where after drinks we agree to a primitive contest.
Preparing for it, you
Scar your face grotesquely with a razor blade.

Upon return, I burn for you my manuscript.
For me you smash your files. I wreck my mother's house.
You wreck your only daughter's mind.

In the end, I write a letter saying:
I forgive you. But you do not write back.
It is now the time for silence.

For we are friends. We love each other very much.

Agape

(after the poem by César Vallejo)

I won't say anyone comes here and asks.
They haven't this afternoon
Asked me for anything much. Nothing!

Not one leper presented himself.
I haven't today
Kissed my quota of sores.

In so fine a parading of lights, I haven't
Seen a single burial flower.
Lord, Lord: I've died so little today,

I'm sorry, forgive me. Everybody goes by
But nobody asks for a thing.
Mal, mal in my hands, like a *cosa ajena.*

If you've mislaid it it's here!
Well, I've gone to the door & I've shouted.
How many doors get slammed in my face!

Something *ajeno ajeno* roots in my soul
And I don't tell you somebody comes here & asks.
Lord, Lord: I've died so little today.

Double Derivation, Association, and Cliché: from *The Great Tournament Roll of Westminster*

I

The heralds wear their tabards correctly.
Each, in his left hand, carries a wand.
Before and after the Master of Armour
Enter his men: three of them carry the staves.
The mace bearer wears a yellow robe.
In right & goodly devysis of apparyl
The gentlemen ride.
The double-curving trumpets shine.

Who breaks a spear is worth the prize.

II

Or makes a forest in the halls of Blackfriars
at Ludgate whych is garneychyd wyth trees & bowes,
wyth bestes and byrds; wyth a mayden
syttyng by a kastell makyng garlonds there;
wyth men in woodwoos dress,
wyth men of armes. . . .
     Or Richard Gibson
      busy
with artificers and labour, portages and ships:
busy with his sums and his accounts:
for what is wrought by carpenters & joyners,
karrovers & smiths . . .
(Who breaks a spear is worth the prize)
Who breaks a schylld on shields
a saylle on sails
a sclev upon his lady's sleeves;
who can do skilfully the spleter werke,
whose spyndylles turn

Power out of parsimony, feasting
Out of famine, revels out of revelation:—
Out of slaughter, ceremony.
When the mist lifts over Bosworth.
When the mist settles on Flodden.

Who breaks a spear is worth the prize.

III

The double-curving trumpets shine:
     & cloth of gold.
The challengers pass . . .

Well, & the advice of Harry Seven:—
(or the Empress Wu, depending
where you are):
We'll put on elegance later.
We'll put off art.
No life of Harry the Seven
     there in the works of the Bard . . .
(No Li Po on Wu)
An uninteresting man? Parsimonious.

Wolsey travels in style . . .
     & on the Field of Cloth of Gold
     & in the halls at Ludgate
a little style. . . .
Something neo-Burgundian
(Holy, Roman, & bankrupt) illuminating
Burgkmairs in *Der Weisskunig & Freydal.*
Rival Maximilian's mummeries, his
dances and his masques, his
armouries & armourers the mark.
Hammermen to King, his prize; King
to hammermen: guard, for love of progeny,
the private parts!
     (My prick's bigger
than *your* prick, or Maxi's prick,
or James')

IV

          & like the Burgkmairs
these illuminations:—
where, o years ago, say twenty-two or
say about five hundred,
cousins in the summertime would
ritualize their rivalries
in sumptuous tableaux.
Someone holds a camera. Snap.
In proper costume, Homo Ludens wears
Imagination on his sleeve.

But chronicle & contour fashion
out of Flodden nothing but the truth.
The deaths, in order & with dignity,
of every child: I remember that.

Who breaks a spear is worth the prize.

V

Who breaks a schylld on shields
          a saylle on sails
a sclev upon his lady's sleeves . . .
And in the north, & for the nearer rival.
Who meteth Coronall to Coronall, who beareth
a man down:—down the distance to Westminster,
down the distance in time.

For the pupil of Erasmus,
for the rival of the Eighth,
a suitcase dated Flodden full of relics.
Shipped Air France, they're scattered
at the battle of the Somme.
It intervened, the news:
it intervenes

As, at the Bankside, Henry makes
a masque at Wolsey's house and, certain
cannons being fired, the paper
wherewith one of them is stopped

does light the thatch, where being
thought at first but idle smoke,
it kindles inwardly consuming
in the end
the house
the Globe

The first & happiest hearers of the town
among them, one Sir Henry Wotton

Largely Fletcher's work

VI

O, largely spleter werke
that certain letters could be sent
unto the high & noble excellent Princess
the Queen of England from her dear & best beloved
Cousin Noble Cueur Loyall with knowledge of
the good and gracious fortune of the birth
of a young prince:
                    & to accomplish certain
feats of arms the king (signed Henry R)
does send four knights . . .

        & sends to work his servant Richard Gibson
on the Revels and Accounts
& sends the children in the summertime to play
& sends the rival Scott a fatal surrogate
from Bosworth, makes an end
to *his* magnificence.

Slaughter out of ceremony, famine
out of feasting, out of power
parsimony, out of revels
revelation . . .

        As an axe in the spine can reveal,
    as an arrow in the eye.

Who breaks a spear is worth the prize.

VII

And what is wrought by carpenters & joyners,
by karrovers & smiths, is worth the prize;
and what is wrought by labour.
For those who play. Of alldyr pooles & paper,
whyght leed and gleew, yern hoopes of sundry
sortes; kord & roopes & naylles:—
All garneychyd at Ludgate. With
trees & bows. All garneychyd with
cloth of Gold.

                    The challengers pass

And deck themselves outrageously
in capes & plumes and armour . . .
And out to play: making in the summertime
a world against all odds, and with
its Winter dangers.

                In a garden, old men play at chess.
                In the Summer. In the Winter, still.

Who will decorate the golden tree,
Employ properly the captive giant
And the dwarf? Who will plead
His rights despite decrepitude . . . ?

                I reach for words as in a photograph
                I reach for costumes in a trunk:

An ancient trunk (an ancient book)

                a saylle, a schylld, a sclev

                a yellow robe, a wand—

pipes & harpes & rebecs,
lutes & viols for a masque.

Where double-curving trumpets shine
The challengers pass.

Who breaks a spear is worth the prize.

Clarifications for Robert Jacoby

("Double Derivation . . .", Part IV, ll. 1-10;
Part VII, ll. 1-15, 22-28)

A moment ago, Robert, I thought I was watching
　　a wren, the one which nests
By my window here, fly, dipping & rising,
　　across this field in Suffolk
So like the one we used to play in, in Ohio,
　　when we were boys. But it was
Really something that you, Dr Jacoby, would
　　be able to explain by pointing out
To me in some expensive, ophthalmological text
　　the proper Latin words.

It was no wren (still less the mythological bird
　　I might have tried to make it)—
But just defective vision: one of those spots
　　or floating motes before the eyes
That send one finally to a specialist. Not
　　a feathered or a golden bird,
Nothing coming toward me in the early evening
　　mist, just a flaw, as they say,
In the eye of the beholder.

Like? in a way?
　　the flaw in the printer's eye
(the typesetter's, the proof-
　　reader's) that produced and then
Let stand that famous line
　　in Thomas Nashe's poem about the plague,
"Brightness falls from the air",
　　when what he wrote was, thinking
Of old age and death, "Brightness
　　falls from the *hair*".

I wonder if you remember all those games
　　we used to play: the costumes,
All the sticks & staves, the whole complicated
　　paraphernalia accumulated to suggest

Authentic weaponry and precise historical dates,
     not to mention exact geographical places,
All through August and September—the months you
     visited. You wanted then, you said,
To be an actor, and your father—a very practical
     lawyer—said he found that funny, though
I think we both intuited
     that he was secretly alarmed.

With little cause. You were destined—how obvious
     it should have been!—to be professional,
Respectable, and eminent. Still, you put in time
     and played your child's part
With skill and grace.

There is a photograph of us taken, I believe,
     in 1950. Your plumed hat (a little
Tight) sits sprightly on your head, your cape
     (cut from someone's bathrobe) hangs
Absurdly down your back, and in your hand you
     brandish the sword of the patriarch
Himself, grandfather M., Commander in Chief
     Of the United Spanish War Vets.
                                    My
Plumed hat is slightly better fitting, if less
     elegant, my sword a fencing foil with
A rubber tip, my cape the prize: something from
     the almost legitimate theatre, from
My father's role in a Masonic play where he spoke,
     once each year before initiations
On some secret, adult stage, lines he practiced
     in the kitchen all the week before:
Let the jewelled box of records be opened
     and the plans for the wall by the
South west gate be examined!

The photographer, it seems, has irritated us.
     We scowl. The poses are not natural.
Someone has said Simon says stand here, look
     there, dress right, flank left;
Someone, for the record, intervenes. Or has
     James arrived? Our cousin from the

East side of Columbus who, with bicycles
      and paper routes and baseballs
Wanted you in time as badly then as I could
      want you out of it. A miniature
Adult, he looked askance at our elaborate
      rituals. He laughed outright,
Derisively. No mere chronicler, he was reality
      itself. I hated him.

Of whom I would remind myself when asking you:
      do you remember? a world of imagination,
Lovely and legitimate, uncovering, summer after
      summer, a place that we no longer go,
A field we do not enter now, a world one tries
      to speak of, one way or another,
In a poem. Robert! Had the jewelled box
      of records been opened and the plans
For the wall by the south west gate been examined,
      news: that he, not you and I, made
Without our knowledge, without our wigs and
      epaulets, with bricks he had a right
To throw, binding rules for our splendid games.

How remote it all must seem to you who joined
      him with such dispatch. One day, I
Suppose, I'll come to you in California saying
      to you frankly: cure me if you can.
Or to some other practicing your arts. Until then,
      what is there to talk about except
This book of photographs? And what they might
      have made of us, all those aunts,
Clucking at our heels, waddling onto Bosworth field
      or Flodden with their cameras. And why
They should have come, so ordinary and so mortal,
      to bring back images like this one
Turning yellow in a yellow book. Brightness fell
      from the hair

Of whom I would be worthy now, of whom I think
      about again as just outside my window
A child plays with a stick. And jumps on both feet
      imitating, since she sees it in the field

(With a stick in its beak), a wren. She enters
        the poem as she enters the field. I will
Not see her again. She goes to her world of stick
        and field and wren; I go to my world
Of poem. She does not know it, and yet she is here:
        here in the poem as surely as there
In the field, in the dull evening light, in the world
        of her imagining, where, as the mist descends,
She is a wren.

As I write that down she is leaving the field.
        She goes to her house where her
Father and mother argue incessantly, where
        her brother is sick. In the house
They are phoning a doctor. In the poem—
        because I say so,
                        because I say once more
That she enters the world of her imagining
        where, as the mist descends,
She is a wren—
        She remains in the field.

Poem for Cynouai

I

With urgency and passion you argue for the lot—
every one of thirty watercolors
ranged in retrospective
which I thought to choose among.
Circumspect, I sought
negotiations. You squint your lazy eye
and wave your arm in arcs
around our geocentric circle and insist:
"We'll take them all!"

II

I am easily persuaded.
How luminous their rendering of a world
we both believe in
and can sometimes share:—
where names are properties of things
they name, where stones
are animate and wilful, trees
cry out in storms, and compulsive
repetition of the efficacious formulae
will get us each his way.

When they patched your overcompensating eye
your work began. Your starboard
hemisphere was starved for colors
and for shapes.
Suddenly a punning and holistic
gnostic, you painted
everything in sight:
your left eye flashed at cats & camels
in the clouds, while one by one

you drew them with a shrewd right hand
into a white corral.
At school they said your "problem"
was "perceptual".

III

What did you perceive,
and what did I?
I found that scattering of words
in notes. I wrote it down
two years ago and now you do not paint.
I no longer wrote. It's out
of date, we've changed.
I was going to quote Piaget
and go on to talk about perception.
Instead I went to work
and earned some money, girl.
I was going to call
you *child.*

Two years, then. We'll keep it honest
as I wander back with you
to Shelford. Bob & Earlene live in Shelford
now, Leif and Luke and Kristin.
Bob has poems in which
he whispers *child, child.*
"We'll take them all," you said,
and I said
I am easily persuaded.
We took just one.

IV

But it is altogether marvelous.
I've kept it here while
you've gone riding with your friends.
Your passion now is horses.
It feels as if you've been away two years—
two years.
Stout-hearted Moshe,

peering one-eyed through your
horse's ears, this bright Ikon that
you've left me makes me
think of William Blake's *Glad Day*.
One sad poet wrote: My
daughter's heavier. And another:
O may she be beautiful, but
not *that* beautiful. I have a friend
who's visited Ms Yeats—
She's bald with warts! O daughters
and their bright glad days
growing beautiful or heavier or bald.
O foolish leers and Lears.

We played. And we play now, but
not so much. Our problem
was perceptual. I think we were
perhaps too Japanese:
I have it on authority
that formal speech retains
the spirit of *bushido* in Japan.
In the *asobase-Kotoba*
we don't say: "I'm here in Shelford"
or "You're riding"
but: "I pretend to be in Shelford"
and "You play at
going riding." Nor does one say:
"I hear your father's dead,"
but this instead:
"I understand your father
has played dying."

V

When my father finished playing dying
I began.
You gave me pictures
which I held against a wound.
I wrote: "How luminous their rendering
of a world we both believe in"
and then I think you stopped believing. . . .

For money, with a friend,
I helped to translate Lars Norén
who far away
in dark, cold Sweden wrote:

Today I see that my daughter
is higher, greater
than I, and completed . . . Her
hard kaiser head encircles me & carries
me and helps me. Silently
we speak in each other—Then
she paves the dead ones.
She comes towards me in her kaiser skirt.

How I stumbled after you with memories & books.
How far ahead you rode. How very
quickly all the books
were closed. How frightening the horses are

As you approach me on The Black Duke of Norfolk.
The Duke's Funeral Helm is low on your eyes
(I stole it for you from a golden nail
in Framlingham church).
Your Ming Dynasty jodhpurs cling to your legs,
cling to your horse's sides
(I sent for them express to Rajasthan).
Your Dalai Lama coat is zipped up tight
(I zipped it up myself).
Your green Tzarina vest divests me.
Your beady Pony Club badge is a third eye
pinned to your cheating heart.
On a velvet photograph of Princess Anne
you are riding in circles of dust.
One eye is patched, old pirate,
and the other eye is glazed.
Only the third one, the Pony Club badge,
can see me, and it stares,
fiery and triumphant.
You are riding in circles of dust.
You are riding into the eye of the Pony Club badge.

First they patched your eye
and then I saw.
My problem was perceptual.

Lars Norén concludes:
She hungers after herself. . . .

VI

What I had wanted to say was: *red, ocher,*
orange, blue, green, violet.
What I had wanted to say was: *grass, sky,*
sun, moon, child, forest, sea.
I had wanted to say: *English village.*
I had wanted to say:
English village a long time ago. . . .
What I had wanted to hear
was the music of flutes and recorders
in a summer garden—
flutes and recorders and tambourines. . . .

What I had wanted to see was light
filtering through the trees
deep in a forest near the sea
where elves and children play together
and adults sip tea
by an enormous ornamented samovar
in solemn conversation
on the nature of the games
the elves & children play. . . .
What I had wanted to write was
love, immortal, laughter, wings. . . .
What I had wanted to do
was to walk forever into a vision
painted by my daughter.
I had wanted her to take me with her there.
I had wanted her
to close the door behind us. . . .

Made of blues and ochers, greens,
made of sunrise and of grass & sky & trees—
Which will be the day
that you remember, child,
when I am only soul-stuff
and can no more enjoy this awkward body
which, despite its ills,
manages to do extraordinary simple things
like walk through heaths of gorse
with you before the others are awake
as the sun comes over
the edge of the earth the ships fall off of
as they tilt on their keels
and roll on the world's last wave. . . .

I remember a day: the rowboat rocked
in the reeds:
my father watched his line. All
the night before we had slept together
in a shack waiting for the dawn.
We didn't talk for hours. He, for once,
was beautifully distracted from
what he always called "the difficult business
of living." There was
no past, there was no future there
in those reeds . . .
                        we were adrift in time,
in timelessness
and no one said we must return—

nor did we sail over any edge of any earth.

Or again: near the house of my childhood
on a street called Glen Echo Drive
there was a tree, an oak,
where my father swung me in a swing—
his long thin fingers
and his firm damp palms on the small of my back
I feel still—
and my bare & grimy feet going up through the leaves!

Mosses grow between his fingers now
and along his palms.
Mosses grow in his mouth & under his arms.
When he finished playing dying
I began. . . .
You gave me pictures
which I held against a wound.
I wrote: *How luminous their rendering* as

You came toward me saying *muzzle, poll, crest,*
withers, loins, croup, dock . . .
As you came saying *snaffle, whip, spurs,*
pommel, cantle, girth.

VIII

And so I try to learn new words
like any child—
I say *flank, hock, heel, hoof;*
I say *fetlock, gaskin, thigh, stifle, sheath.*
I would meet you now
according to my bond. I try to put away
this Ikon which sustained me.
I write *Equitation: Mounting & dismounting.*
Circumspect, I seek
negotiations. I wave my arms
around in frantic circles and insist:
"I'll learn them all"
while you ride off on paths
through fields of gorse and into sunsets
which are not even slightly picturesque—

While you ride off in hurricanes of dust.

—Just one time were three of us together:
father, father-son, and daughter.
We played at something, riding, painting,
poetry, or dying—
it hardly matters what . . .
And at our playing
                    —(while, perhaps,

someone picked a mandolin
and strangers talked about us solemnly
around an ornamented samovar
and sipped their tea)—
our lines of vision crossed
and then we started changing places painfully. . . .

The child is father of the man
but not the child the poet meant.
The child of flesh and blood
and not the ghost of former selves
is father of the man—
The Daughter on the Black Duke of Norfolk
She
is father of the man
The Daughter
Who is Higher, Greater & Completed
She
is father of the man
The Daughter on the Black Duke of Norfolk
The one who made the picture
the one who gave the gift
the one who paved the dead
the one who wore the patch
the one who was Japanese
the one who learned to ride a horse
And Hungers After Herself—

She
is father of the man
The daughter on the Black Duke of Norfolk

The one whose problem was perceptual

The one who rides away

And the Manual says: *It is interesting to assess the progress and accuracy of the training by riding a circle on ground upon which the imprints of the horse's hoofs can be seen.* . . .

(1974–1977)

IV

East Anglian Poem

I

Materials of Bronze and of Iron—

  linch-pins and chariot wheels, nave-bands
and terret-rings: harness mounts, fittings, and
bridle-bits: also a sword, an axe: also a
golden torc
           But the soils
           are acid here

           and it rains

Often there's only the mark of a tool on a bone
Often there's nothing at all

II

They herded oxen and sheep   They hunted the deer
They made a simple pottery, spun yarn   They scratched
in the earth to little effect
               They were afraid

     of him

    here, with his armour

        thigh and skull unearthed
          beside the jawbone of his horse

Afraid of him who
    feared these others, Belgae,
speaking Celtic too, but building oppida, advancing,
turning sod with coulters and with broad-bladed ploughs.
      (Caesar thought them civilized—
          which meant familiar

They minted coins

They made war on a sophisticated scale)

III

Sub Pellibus:

    Rectangular tents in orderly lines
and round the camp a ditch.
    Palisade stakes. Rows of javelins
with soft iron shanks, the semi-
    cylindrical shields.

        Second Augusta here—
    with auxilia: archers and slingers,
            mercenary Gauls.

He saw them on parade:

    their elegant horses, their leathers
studded with gilt, their silvered pendants and
the black niello inlay of their fittings
    and their rings

    their helmets made an apparition
of the face: apertures for eyes. Their
jerkins were embroidered, their yellow plumes and
    scarlet banners sailed in the wind.

    So they'd propitiate their gods.

He saw them on parade:

    to his north and east
the boundary was the sea
    iron pikes were driven
in the Waveney and Yare
    to his west the fenlands
forest to the south
    and south as well
between the trees and fens

at Wandlebury here
along a narrow belt of chalk
   no more than eight
miles wide

        his ramparts rose

        (where certain grave-goods lie)

IV

Within his hornworks
Behind his stone and timber walls
Below his towers and beneath his ample crop

      these early dead

           (he saw the Trinovantes destroyed
           who later saw Caratacus in chains)

      Their armlets and their
      toe-rings still adorn. Bronze
      bowls, amphorae, still provide.

       . . . and magic tokens there
      and writings there corrupted.
      With all their stolen coins,
      a carnyx there to play.

      And stood up in the marshes many days.
      Nor cried for meat.
      Nor longed for any cup.

Consider what they were before
that men could suffer labour.

And feed upon the roots and barks of trees.

V

Before him and unknown to him and
southward came the stones: dolerite-blue
with tiny bits of felspar. From the Mt Prescelly
outcrops—Carn Meini, Foel Trigarn

"Lord, and you must climb the holy peak"

Before him and unknown to him
the first charioteers
Before him, the first tamer of horses.

He saw the hare run
toward the sun, the

mistletoe and sickle
in the tree

From the woods and the bogs
they began to assemble

After the flat-bottom boats in the shallows of Mona

VI

After the incantations and the libations
After the auguries in the grove of the dishonored queen
After the spectral bride at the mouth of the Thames

Did the tethered swans fly above him?
Did the deer follow behind?

And after the pounding of magic into the swords?

From the confiscated lands
From the Calendar of Rites
From the Forward Policy of Rome

From the open hands of
    frightened and obsequious client-kings
From the pride of the Legatus
From the procurator's greed

        From the Divine House of Tiberius Claudius
           His octastyle temple and His Name
        NUMEN AUGUSTI
           From the hands of the Goddess of Death

The tethered swans flew above him
And the deer followed behind

The Noble Art of Fence: A Letter

Ardent fight stayeth a gardant fight
    or putteth backe
    or beateth
Open fight stayeth an open fight
Variable answereth variable
Close fight is beaten by gardant fight

Slowfoot: swift hand   Quickfoot: slow hand

    tread, stride, follow, fallaway

    . . . they seek a true defense in an untrue sword.Rapiers!
Frogpricking poniards! The strange devices of Italians and the French.
Toys fit to murder poultrie, I should say.
My Lord:
        THEY BRING THEIR LIVES
TO AN END BY ART

        Can they pierce a corslet
            or unlace a helmet strap?
        Can they hew asunder pikes?

     tempestuous terms
        stocata, dritta, reversa

     our best men fall to style.

Speak not evil? Behind the backs of Men? Dispraise no play nor workmanship?
But Italians! We answer the bragging strangers,
we point: Signior Rocko and Signior Rocko
his son

     with false play or plaine
     with broken shins, cracktpates.

. . . for Rocko came to town all right and built himself a fancy place in War-wicke Lane. Not a fencing-school, mind you, but a *college*. Styled himself the World's Greatest Master Of The Art. (And teaching *offense!*) His scholars—noblemen and gen-tlemen of the court—would set up their arms: and under these their gear: rapiers and daggers, gloves of mail and gauntlets . . . He was the darling of the sycophants and courtiers: much beloved by men who never need to draw a sword, men of elegance and wit, men of leisure, poets: men who can afford a fashion or a style. One day Austen Bagger being merrie and amongst his friends, took his Sword and Buckler and his valiant heart off to Warwick Lane, and standing there upon his skill he shouted: ROCKO, YOU FAG-GOT, UP YOUR ASS WITH BOATMEN'S OARS AND BATTLE AXE AND PIKE. UP YOUR ASS WITH RAPIERS . . .

> And down came Rocko with his two hand sword
> And manfully did Austen Bagger close with him
> And stroke up his heels
> And cut him under the breech . . .

Shall I admonish against quarrels and brawls?
I tell you: Judgment, Distance; Time & Place & Measure
I do not darkly ryddle here
I set it down

I choose, my Lord,
    the short and ancient weapons of our land.

The times are difficult, and have been. I tell you plainly that our Masters of Defense are thought by those who flatter Bobadill to be so many vagabonds and bearwards. The city fathers, fearing, as they say, the plague, will have no prizes played in London. But any haberdasher sells to any cobbler bucklers. Every serving man will play with hilted cudgels squawking in the language of Italian schools. But Richard Beste? Gunner at the Tower. William Hearne? Yeoman of the guard. William Joyner? Tavern keeper. John Evans? Jerkin-maker. Honest men and masters of a mystery, but all of them pretending trades because the Law from Coke and Blackstone on has always here and still will threaten penalties . . .

I mean the Statute of Rogues
I mean the Vagrancy Act
I mean to say I'm not among the lewd and dissolute who'd
    covet singular advantage without license or authority or oath

I'd teach a man to fight!

So here's
our bargain Sir
and guild or no incor-
poration patent royal favour
ipso facto lawful sworn I swear it
on a hilt which is to say the cross KNOW
YE THAT WE admit all provosts of sufficient
cunning expert tried before us masters of the science
openly within the city giving scholars first a warning twenty
days and then to playe their prize by god or sovereign lady queen
of england france and ireland all her sherifbaylif's deputies and con-
stables we certify commission and we license deputize defenders of the realm

of england by the grace of god amen

The weapons are not rapiers.The weapons are the longsword sword and buckler
backsword sword and dagger stave or pike the great two-handed sword the single dagger
javelin the partisan the black bill glaive and half-pike battle axe . . .

and these are times:

The time of the hand
The time of the hand and bodie
The time of the hand, bodie and foot

The time of the foot
The time of the foot and bodie
The time of the foot, bodie and hand

. . . This is not mathematics this is movement. This is not manners: This is not ballet.
Whatsoever is done with the hand before the foot or feet is true.Whatsoever is done with
the foot or feet before the hand is false. I tell you: Judgment, Distance; Time & Place &
Measure. I tell you grips and wrestlings. I tell you thrusts and blows. Treading of ground,
doubles, wards, closing and breaking, knees to the groin, boot in the ass, knife in the eyes:
There *is* no observation of Italian niceties in War.

And now there are more of them.
I mean Saviolo and Co.

Business is bad . . .

. . . our poets advertise their doings on the stage and yet not one of them will play his prize. They stay indoors and write their books and talk of etiquette. They read Castiglione, draw their diagrams from Euclid, darn their hose, inspire all diversities of lies. All of them are pederasts. They dance the galliard and pavane, they vault most nimbly, oh they caper loftily these warlike souls who translate greek and perish from the French disease . . .

Hieronimo, go by. Well *he* got *his* at least.

They'll touch the weapons of another man that weareth them yet deal with all punctilio to be observed. They talk of noble ancestors in Rome . . .

> They boast outrageously
> > They dye their beards
> They only feign
> > They will not fight

These euphuistic lurid sodomites . . .

TAKE UP FENCING! Drive away all aches and pains; drive away disease and grief, make a nimble body, get thee strength. It sharpeneth the wit, expelleth choler, melancholy, many other vile conceits: it keepeth man in breath, in perfect health, it makes him to be long of life who useth it . . . Item, item, item! You shall swear so help you god that you shall uphold and maintain such articles as shall be here delivered unto you . . . Item, item, item! Loving truth and hating falsehood you shall be a master to the last day of your life. Item, item, item! You shall not any suspect person teach, no murderer nor common quarreler no drunkard no nor shall you mix with them . . .

> You shall be merciful.
> You shall love and honor him who taught you cunning.

> item, item, item . . .

> > *useless!*

I weep for master Turner: murdered with a pistol from behind.
I weep for Henry Aldington: hanged.
I weep for Furlong: drunk a pint of aqua vita straight off
> in one go; then he fell down dead.
I weep for Westcott: suicide

> . . . for there are wicked angels which are waiters
and attend upon ungodly life . . . attend upon

                    the time of the hand
                        the time of the hand and bodie
                    the time of the hand, bodie and foot

        . . . and then he need not fear to say Come Quickly: today or tomorrow,
or when thou wilt, and with what manner of death soever,
so it come by thine appointment . . .

            l think I'll go get Saviolo myself.
            I'll challenge him, call him out of his
            Elegant house, away from his elegant friends.

            I'll close with him. I'll strike up his heels.
            I'll cut him under the breech.
            I'll take his scalp. I'll take his scalp.

            I'll vanish quick (quick!) to Illyria.

A Cambridge Spinning-House:
Henry John Temple Palmerston's Syllabics
For Marianne Moore

I too dislike it
   but the matron shall have
no occupation or calling but that
   of matron
of the house She shall reside
   on the premises
and not
   be absent for a night without permssion

I too dislike it
   but she shall cause a print
ed copy of the rules respecting the
   inmates to
be hung up in every cell
   and shall read or cause
to be
   read the said rules to every inmate upon

her commital I
   too dislike it She shall
learn these rules herself and observe them well
   and as far
as possible cause them to
   be observed by all
I too
   dislike it but she must enter in her book

everything that she
   sees and hears She shall rule
her roost and exercise her authori
   ty with firm
ness temper and humani
   ty and abstain from
language
   and remarks that might be seen as calcula

ted to irritate
            an inmate She shall at
tend to the employments and industri
            al training
of inmates follow the di
            rections of the chap
lain with
            regard to their instruction and assist by

her influence and
            authority his ex
ertions for their reformation I too
            dislike it
The cells she must visit and
            frequently inspect
also the
            yard kitchen and other parts of the house She

shall occasional
            ly go through the house at
an uncertain hour of the night and re
            cord in her
journal the hour of the vis
            it and the state of
the house
            at the time She shall see the inmates locked up

at night in their cells
            at eight o'clock and shall
have the gate of the house locked and the key
            placed in safe
keeping She shall enforce a
            high degree of clean
liness
            in every part of the house and also in

the persons of the
            inmates their clothing bed
ding and everything in use She shall take
            every pre
caution against the escape
            of an inmate and

she shall
        examine the windows doors bars bolts and locks

I too dislike it
        but the inmates shall keep
their cells and the furniture and uten
        sils therein
clean and in good order They
        shall be clean and neat
in their
        persons wash their hands and faces daily and

wash their feet or bathe
        at least once a week or
as often as the matron shall direct
        No inmate
shall disobey the orders
        of the matron or
other
        officers of the house or treat with disre

spect any of the
        officers or servants
or any person visiting the house
        or employed
therein or be idle or
        negligent in her
work or
        wilfully damage the same or absent her

self without leave from
        divine service or the
daily prayers or behave irreverent
        ly thereat
or be guilty of any
        indecent or im
moral
        language or conduct or use any provok

ing or abusive
        words or converse or hold
intercourse with any other inmate

in a way
not authorized by the rules
of the house or cause
annoy
ance or disturbance by singing or making

a noise or pass or
attempt to pass out of
her cell or beyond the bounds of the room
or place where
she may be employed or dis
figure the walls or
other
parts of the house or deface secrete destroy

or pull down any
paper or notice hung
up by authority in or about
the house or
wilfully injure any
clothing bedding or
other
article or commit any nuisance or

have in her cell or
possession any ar
ticle not furnished by the establish
ment or give
or lend to or borrow from
any other in
mate an
y food book or other article without

leave or refuse or
neglect to conform to
the rules regulations and orders of
the house The
matron may examine an
y inmate touching
such of
fences and determine thereupon and may

cause any inmate
      so offending to be
punished by being closely or other
      wise confined
in a dark or light cell or
      dislike it dislike
it I
      too dislike it dislike it I too dislike

*I certify the foregoing Rules as proper
to be enforced in the Spinning-House at Cambridge.*

Whitehall, 21 Feb. 1854. PALMERSTON.

Mr. Rothenstein's Rudiments

It's strange. I told that pretty girl yesterday
that, yes, I knew her mother, but I knew her
great-grandmother too—Lady Burne-Jones.
It's even stranger, thinking on it, that I met
Rossetti's brother as a child; I can see
him clearly lying on that couch I rescued
for the Tate—the one on which the poet's friends
placed Shelley's body when they took it from the sea—
when I heard the house, Rossetti's, took a hit
during the blitz.
                    My father knew them all, of course—
Sir William! Whistler and Degas, Rodin, Pater,
Swinburne, Henry James. After the Slade he went
to Paris and he might have stayed,
except that Basil Blackwood, then at Balliol,
commissioned him to make that portrait drawing
that initiated the entire Oxford series
published by John Lane. So home he came and
grew more earnest reading Tolstoy, speaking
much of Probity. A French Benedictine,
and later also Eric Gill, thought
he should enter an order, or anyway go paint
at Ditchling Common. He stayed in London, though,
and met Augustus John and all the younger men.
As the influence of Whistler waned, his line began
to grow a little thick, his canvasses
just a little cluttered.

Augustus John. And Gwen. Do you realize
we nearly had Gwen John in Bronze on the embankment?
Every time I stand before the *Burghers of Calais*
I see poor Gwen. She posed for Rodin when he did
the plaster for a Whistler monument, holding
a medallion of her teacher. But because it lacked an arm—
I'd guess that half his figures lack an arm or leg—
the jury opted for a casting of the *Burghers* and

Augustus found his sister, after she had died, leaning
back against a wall in some obscure dark corner
of a Paris shed. I mean of course he found
the *plaster* of his sister . . .

        . . . Anyone who'd say that Stanley Spencer
is inferior to Arp or Mondrian can't see!
Everybody followed Fry and then got stuck somehow
on all those formal theories and by what
you'd have to call an orthodoxy after being bowled away
by Post-Impressionism. Give me Stanley Spencer
to a watered-down Matisse by Duncan Grant.
Besides, his character's of interest.
And the more we know about him and the world
he inhabited the more we see in what he made.
I'd say that's true of any artist. Also we can sometimes
understand the way a man can fill his art with
all the qualities and virtues that his life most lacks—
And that's a knowledge I prefer to Mr. Fry's
aesthetics and to all the revolutions of a Herbert Read.

Stanley! He came one night to dinner, missed
his train to Cookham, and then stayed on
for something like three months. He'd talk all day,
all night: Cookham and his painting.
His father read the bible to his children every night
and every morning Stanley walked through Cookham
seeing all the stories re-enacted in his village
by the Thames. In a way, he really did believe
they had occurred there—Jerusalem,
The emanation of his Cookham youth!
Look at his *Nativity,* his *Zacharias and Elizabeth.*
When I acquired the *Resurrection* for the Tate,
half of London sneered, half the critics
simply thought him crazy. Then they condescended,
calling him "a village pre-Raphaelite"—Spencer,
whose *Zacharias* I'd be willing to compare
even with Giotto . . .
                    He did travel a bit after the war—
as far as China once. When Chou En-Lai remarked
he hoped these English now would know New China,
Stanley said he hoped New China might one day
know Cookham. . . .

Wyndham Lewis
didn't come from Cookham—
much more likely Mars. He arrived in London
like some trigger-happy extraterritorial
and took on everything and everyone in sight.
He was, he'll probably remain, a mystery.
I knew him pretty well. And yet he'd be so
secretive he wouldn't even let you know he had
a wife after he'd been married several years.
She'd make the dinner for her husband and a guest,
set the table, then just disappear . . .

Of course it was the Fry affair, the mess
at the Omega, that was much responsible
for Lewis's mistreatment by the crowd
that wanted to control a nation's taste.
He claimed that Fry had stolen his commission
to design a sitting-room for the *Daily Mail's*
model home exhibit, then in compensation offered
him an overmantel where he'd be allowed
to execute a carving. So Lewis sent that letter
to the press about a *timid but voracious*
journalistic monster that finished him with
Bloomsbury and Fry. But in an age of log-rolling,
as he said himself, Mr. Lewis
never once was rolled . . .

Do you realize
that no one ever had convincingly portrayed
an ordinary business suit before the Lewis *Eliot?*
I mean with full verisimilitude, without
somehow ennobling it. There sits the poet—
in the suit he'd worn at Lloyds!

The editor of *Blast* and the friend of Ezra Pound
went to war in the artillery, then came home
and painted *Bagdad, Barcelona, Stations of the Dead.*
He said his geometrics wanted filling
and he filled them with inventions, not
with the matter of the continental Cubists.
I heard him say of Braque that one might very well
be musical or vegetarian, but life was more
than mandolins and apples.

                              And more (or maybe less!)
than all those decorations on the walls
at Charleston as well, that strange domestic
Sistine Chapel down in Sussex. I thought I'd better
go there and make my peace with Mrs. Bell
when I decided I should write on Duncan Grant.
It was not a happy visit.
I guess I said that it was my opinion
Titian couldn't draw. Anyway, she glared at me
as if I'd shot the gun that killed her son in Spain.
I've tried to do an honest job on Grant—
mainly as a decorator and the artist
of the Holland portrait and the two of Mrs. Bell.
Still, it's difficult to make ambitious claims for him
like those put forward by his friends—

and also difficult, sitting there at Charleston,
the light pouring on a garden full of flowers and
through a window on the decorated walls, the pottery,
the accumulations of a privileged life, not to think
about a painter like Gwen John, isolated and unknown,
or of my father as his reputation steadily declined
and he sat alone on the terrace at Far Oakbridge
gazing at the contours of the valley in his illness,
looking through the beauty of this world
at something he could almost see behind it.

                    (Cento: Passages & paraphrase from John Rothenstein's
                         Modern English Painters. Variation, derivation, &
                         apocrypha)

Rostropovich at Aldeburgh

I: as soloist

The Haydn Concerto in C with Britten's cadenzas:
He flies through these (the cadenzas)
Like an Aeroflot plane, like a Concordski,
Out of the 18th century into our own
And then back.
It's difficult for us to tell
Which of these ages he's happiest in
Or with which composer
Or whether if all of us wore our wigs
And our wings
To tea at the Maltings
We'd feel completely out of our time
Or merely well dressed.

II: as conductor

The Shostakovich 14th.
Which broods on
Death and is eloquent.

His wife, Galina Vishnevskaya,
Sings with Ulrik Cold
The texts by Apollinaire, Lorca,

Küchelbecker, and Rilke.
Which brood on
Death and are eloquent.

The widow of the composer
Sits in the audience.
What we applaud for is what

In each of us might, if we're lucky,
Survive. And he applauds back at us,
Being Russian. He's beaming and

Bouncing, blessing us all with his smile.
He kisses the hand of his wife,
The cheek of the first violinist,

The balding head of every balding
Percussionist:
One, two, three, and four.

III: as teacher

He offers, pianissimo and then fortissimo, pianistically, his parodies in Master Class.
For *their* edification. For *our* amusement. He doesn't touch the cello for a minute. To
play it after Rostropovich plays it on the cello? The piano is enough. He is, when we
arrive, already in full flight. We tiptoe tiptoe in all knowing well the famed benevolence
can turn to rage. He's talking talking talks: to Klaus, a while, a German . . . Oh

too lyrical he says it's *monumental* here just here translation (simultaneous) by lovely
lady former student and some Deutsch from him plus double Dutch and now and
then self-mockery in English teaching with his gestures too expressions pained delight-
ed well he says too soon too much vibrato J.S. Bach's your special intimate or what I
say *respect* he's tapping on his wrist he's tapping on his knee da da da da Da Da Da
Da YES NO is it so very short you think you've got just sixteen bars to play you're
saving nothing *nothing* Klaus to finish with and stricter *shhhhh* conducts and grace
abounding now he likes it now and smiling now and then *disgrace disgraceful* no and
one more time oh play it one more time but better slowly faster now ah bravo bravi
da da da no *Niet* commence again he strings his fingers bows the air makes once
makes twice some arcane long lost sign which has no name and never will in language
Deutsch or Russian English there must be just here he says to end the lesson here he
says just here I say must be a ray of sunshine here he says a ray of sunshine over
everyone ah da.

Lines for the Gentlemen

I

1667. And on Landguard beach, 1000 Dutch.
That was the last invasion.
Afterwards, 1753-66,
Governor Thicknesse, thank you, defending, sir.
(And plenty of out-of-work sailors)

II

And as with piracy, there's honour in it.
And not just honour among thieves—
A rising class will not, they'd tell you,
be put down. Custom?
                                        Brandy! tea, wool, rum,
just name it—
So the word gets round. Someone's
had the pox, someone's
had the plague. All's free trade
at certain cottages where rumored illnesses
or rumored ghosts
keep all but customers away—

Laces for a lady; letters for a spy
And watch the wall, my darling, while the
            Gentlemen go by.

III

This one watched the wall; that one
closed his eyes.
The headless gunner walked on the embankment.

A crescent moon rose smartly from behind
the nasty gibbet. There are
voices in the back room of The Crown—

and Mr. Plumer, MP from Appleby,
speaking in the House
and saying ALL IMPROVEMENT OF THE LAND

HAS BEEN SUSPENDED
while the Parson whispers to his wife
the wages of gin

for our duties
and hides the three enormous tubs
beneath the altar cloth.

4,000,000 gallons of booze are flowing
into England! (Three slow
cutters chasing one fast swipe.)

The publican
has put the spotsmen all to sleep.
Bright lights are flashing

Down the Orwell and the Alde.

More Lines for the Gentlemen

(for L. M., age 6)

I

Thicknesse summons from obscurity
the young Gainsborough

to his Landguard Fort—
The Future's in their hands!

Like muddy Primaveras, there emerge
from busy tidal harbor into history, apotheosis:

Chesterfield and Mrs. Siddons
Pitt & Burke & Clive—

Also, though not on anybody's canvas,
not on anybody's list of invitations,

John Pixley Thomas Fidget Black George
Nichols poor Will Laud

& all
the merry rest of them—

smugglers

II

The Rev. Richard Cobbold, Rector of Wortham & Rural Dean,
writes of Margaret Catchpole's early days:

Who has not seen the healthy face of childhood in those ever interesting years when activity commences? And what philanthropist, delighting in scenes of genuine simplicity and nature, could fail to admire the ruddy glow of youth, and the elastic step of confidence, with which the young female peasant bounds to meet a parent or a brother at the welcome hour of noon. . . .

My youngest female child, genuinely simple,
ruddy in the glow of youth,
elastic of step, confident, bounding to meet

her male parent at the welcome hour of noon,
gets it wrong. She tells her friend,
bounding with philanthropic step behind her:

My dad's writing a book about snuggling.

III

FAMOUS SNUGGLERS OF THE SUFFOLK COAST

On Harwich: Mr Arnott, Master of Rivers: "It was even
considered dangerous to sail across the harbour after dark for
fear of being set upon by snugglers."

At a Screening of Gance's *Napoleon:*
Arts Theatre, Cambridge

In the shadow of the eastern towers of Kings
and in the Sunday-dinner darkened theater where
Lydia Keynes once danced the frozen breath away
from puffing Cambridge dons, we eat our

sandwiches between parts three and four of
Abel Gance's reconstructed, spliced-together,
silent, five-hour epic on Napoleon.
I am, said Bonaparte, *a rock thrown into space.*

We can believe it. Spinning giddily from images
of Corsica to images of storms tossed up by
the Sirocco, the Convention, and Rouget de Lisle,
we'd clutch at almost anything, even this

unfashioned rock that tumbles through the space
of an unfinished film and cries: *to make
yourself well understood, speak to people's eyes!*
Our eyes are red; we rub them in the interval

and stuff our mouths with cheese & chutney, wash
it down with beaujolais kept cool in a thermos.
Somewhere in part two, reel seventeen or so,
beneath the guns of Admiral Hood pounding batteries

outside Toulon where Dugommier attacks the captured
port, Bonaparte assumed command. The silence
of all that exhausted us: this black & white morality
keeps its moral to itself or hasn't got one yet.

Shall we see in Antonin Artaud's Marat, or even
in Maxudian's Barras, the cruel stuff of History?
or do we gape at mysteries of Art? (We might have
left before the Terror if we hadn't brought our

sandwiches and wine.) Abel Gance maintained that
he had made Prometheus. He said (aloud)
he'd found a cinematic style capable of Vision.
Then the markets crashed and Jolson's busy progeny

made all those early talkies sing & pay their way.
War's anachronism, said this hero of the triple screen,
tearing every city down in sight. And Gance:
All those polyvision sequences to come, you've seen.

Ahhhh! we said, watching Cinerama in the fifties,
waiting for the famous rollercoaster ride that actually
made kids throw up their popcorn. These final reels
will march us out beyond the foothills through the Alps,

the screen split into three to make us gasp:
as triptych or as trinity, *Les Mendiants de la Gloire*
will traipse behind Napoleon into Italy—
we'll never see the Empire or a sunset by the Loire.

We'll wait, like Josephine, with spots before our eyes:
those blinking phantoms a machine's already loosed,
the gangling ghosts of Robespierre, Marat,
the feminine, impassioned, & most elegant Saint-Just.

From a Visit to Dalmatia, 1978

I

Korčula is oleander, cypresses & twisted
fig trees; Korčula is stones—
Lemon trees and stones. Quick mirages
above the stones & olive groves:
Shaky vineyard walls of broken stones and

Stones that must be gathered, piled up
before the shallow arbor roots will
take a tenuous hold
in sandy earth: And shallow stony graves
for Partisan or priest, invader.

Limestone & limestone rock in hills
around Lumbarda, limeface of Sveti Ilija
after Orebić:
                 Rockslides and
washed out roads, karst—
a landscape that will break you on its back
or make a sculptor of you—

Lozica, Kršinić, Ivan Jurjević-Knez.

II

Or if not a sculptor then a fisherman.
Or, it would have once.
                         Looking at the empty streets
at noon, Toni Bernidić
tells me it's the woist and hottest
day so far in June—he learned
his English in Brooklyn
during the war—
But his house is cool, and so
are the wines: Grk, Pošip, Dingač. . . .

He tells me of the wooden ships
he built, each one taking
him a year: but well made, well made—
The work, he says,
was heavy—pointing to his tools.

Now he has no work: the island's
income is from tourists
and the flushed young men who'd once
have been apprentices
sport their *Atlas* badges, ride their
scooters to the Park or Marco Polo
or the Bon Repos
and show their muscles to the breezy
blue-eyed girls
whose wealthy fathers order loudly
wiener schnitzel

wienerschnitzel and stones.

A Wind in Roussillon

I

The Tramontane that's blowing pages
of an unbound book through Roussillon
departs on schedules
of its own. . . .

Et nous, les os . . . et nous, les os.
And us, the bones.

II

The train departs from Austerlitz on time.
After Carcassonne, Tuchan,
wheat and barley dry up in the sun
& trees appear hung heavily
with cherries, lemons, oranges.

Red tiled roofs are angled oddly
on the little houses in the hills below Cerdagne.
Gray slate's left behind.

By the tracks
a villager has nailed up a goat's foot
and a sunflower to the door
that opens on his vineyard
circled by a wall of heavy stones.

III

In French, the words of Mme T. about les îles Malouines sound nearly as bizarre as ads
for the religious kitsch at Lourdes translated into English in the same edition of *Le Monde*
. . . "A see-through plastic model of the Virgin with unscrewable gold crown enables you

to fill the image up with holy water from a tap." And Mme T., *qui a félicitée les forces armées,* swells in French to the dimensions of a Bonaparte: *les plus merveilleuses du monde . . . le courage et l'habileté ont donné une nouvelle fierté à ce pays et nous ont fait comprendre que nous étions vraiment une seule famille.*

Et nous, les os: vraiment une seule famille.

IV

Low hills dense with yellow broom!
Cactus, thistles, wild mountain roses;
lavender and holly and convolvulus.
Above the rows of plane trees,
olive groves root down through rock.
Above the olive groves, cypresses & pines.

Down the valley under Canigou
a helicopter dips and passes overhead,
circles the Clinique Saint-Pierre
whining like a homing wasp.
Landing in an asphalt parking lot,
it scatters old men playing skittles, boules.
Young men wearing orange flight suits
carry something human
wrapped in white inside.

V

The name of one low, ruined house
in Perpignan is John
and Jeanne. (It's in another country.)
When great winds pass the threshold
nothing sings or appears.

It's John & Jeanne
and from their graying faces
falls the plaster of day. (Far off
the most ancient one,
the arch daughter of shadows.)

You build a fire in the cold great hall
and you withdraw.
(Your name is Yves Bonnefoy.)
You build it there, and you withdraw.

VI

My hostess came to Perpignan from Dublin more than forty years ago. Now in her late sixties, she lives in the third floor flat of an elegant eighteenth-century house in what were once the servants' quarters. The walls are full of books on Cathar heresies and Albigensians and Templars. When the south of France was flayed for twenty years in the Crusades, blood ran all the way from Montségur to the Queribus Château before it finally dried. Mme Danjou came here with the Quakers when the Spanish Civil War broke out and helped Republican refugees across the border at Port Bou. Four years later she was helping Jews across the border in the opposite direction when the Roussillon was occupied by the Nazis. Denounced by a neighbor, she was thrown in jail where she waited for the train that would take her to a prison camp in Germany. Like other European women of her generation, she is tough. "One felt," she says, struggling for a moment with the English that she rarely speaks these days, "that one had work to do." The war had ended by the time the Nazis sent the train.

VII

Not only the delimited circumferences
but also all the white stone houses
in the streets of southern Catholic cemeteries
speak of walled towns by Vauban
or by his foretypes in the Middle Ages or before.
This silent town within the town of Collioure
where Derain and Picasso paid their bills
with paintings no one wanted yet
fortifies itself against the naked bathers
and the tourists at the Templiers.
I intrude upon the silent tenants searching
for Antonio Machado.

The wealthy dead inhabit their expensive homes
and wait impatiently for quick descendants
. to arrive and fill each empty room marked *reservée*.
The poor lie down in dresser drawers stacked high

in marble walls around a central Calvary
and whisper without any *nouvelle fierté à ce pays:*
"Nous étions vraiment une seule famille."

Machado fled from Franco's armies
first to Barcelona, then across the border
with some refugees. Dying, he came
on foot, and in the rain, and with his mother.
He left the room they gave him only once
to walk alone along the streets of Collioure
before they brought him here.
He sings these dead his mortal words forever.
Globo del fuego . . . disco morado . . .

The sun that parched the bones
dries up the town, dries up the southern sea.
Savilla is distant and alone.
Sol. Soleil.
Castile, and Collioure! Machado.

VIII

With knife or nail or glass someone clumsily
has scratched into the blackened wooden gate
that's chained high up beyond one's reach
at Fort Saint-Elme: *Privée, Bien Gardée.*

A small green lizard darts between two stones.
It looks to be deserted in the tower, and yet
it's difficult to tell. Everything inside
has been restored. They say it's lived in now.

Climbing here, I heard two cuckoos answering
each other down the valley. A kestrel hovers high
and drops to earth the far side of the tower.
No sound now but northern wind on fortified étoile.

The level sea below me mirrors Le Château Royal
that Dugommier won back for revolution after
Dufour's treason turned the cannon of Saint-Elme
on quiet Collioure for money and for Spain.

From the col de Banyuls through Port-Vendres
they'd advanced. Then, bien gardée, Saint-Elme.
A captain stood about where I stand, bargaining.
Dufour let him quickly through the gates.

No one sang the cruel cannonade they loosed
on the Château which burned away the Middle Age
from rampart, hall and tower. Dugommier won back
the smoking bones before which once some

pitiful last troubadour sang out to Templars
gazing down at him beside the sea. No one gazes
down from Fort Saint-Elme. Nor do I sing out
Dòna, maries de caritat . . .
                    Lady, mother of charity . . .
I was born too late. . . .

IX

Tour de la Massane, Tour de Madeloc. Towers like these stretch along the backbone of the
Pyrenees and look down on the plain of Roussillon, the southern coast, and Spain. By day
the little garrisons would signal to each other with a puff of smoke, by night with fire.
Valerius Flaccus, Commandant at Madeloc, left his chiselled mark on the great rock. In
Rome, they put him on a coin. In Roussillon, les os. *Que malvaise chançon de nos chanté
ne seit,* he might have said a little later and a little to the west. What he said, in fact, was
this:

VALERIUS FLACCUS
PRAEFECTUS PRAESIDII MONUMENTUM JUSSIT
VIVUS SIBI CONDI LOCO
INTERCEPTO ET EMUNITO

The buried temple spits no mud or rubies out. The sun pours down upon the tower that
now relays the television news from Paris, London, Rome, and even as far off as Las Mal-
vinas or The Lebanon. I sit in my hotel and drink in martial music from the streets of
Buenos Aires. Then we see Israeli tanks annihilate Beirut. Communication is a subtle thing
through our electric sepulchre. In the Punic wars, Valerius could only talk in hyperbolic
terms with smoke and fire. . . . Power hymns instalments to its spirit now in all works of
impatience: wars, towers, rituals, TV. In memory, Valerius, you arise. Like an occult lan-
guage found in an iron-bound book.

X

Mother of charity, Mother of consolation,
Your house is not La Tour Madeloc,
Mother of bones, Mother of dissolution.

Lady of leisure, Lady of Roussillon,
Maître Xinxet has blackened your hermitage,
Lady of landfall, Lady of languors.

Mother of ostentation, Mother of ordure,
Neptune rests in your chapel,
Mother of noon, Mother of nightshade.

Lady of purdah, Lady of purchase,
The village cries out for rain,
Lady of drought, Lady of departures.

Mother of Jesus, Mother of jackals,
The pilgrim is flaying the Jew,
Mother of olives, Mother of obeisance,

Lady binding the book in leather & iron,
Mother of scattered pages,
Work of secret patience, Tramontane.

V

Not having read a single fairy tale

for a long long time
because my children now are grown,
I buy a book of them for the child of friends
and later get caught up in it alone
waiting nervously beside the phone
for word of an adult.

Once there was a cat
who made acquaintance of a rat.
There was a peasant once
who drove his oxen with a heavy load of wood.
An ugly fisherman lived with an ugly wife
in an ugly shack beside the heaving sea.
A man was rich, another man was poor.
A father called his children in before him.
Once there was a little girl
whose mother and father had died.
Once there was a witch.

Time passes. It is late.
Outdoors the wind is howling, and it rains.
My beard turns gray and
grows between my legs, grows
across the carpet, down the basement stairs.
The house creaks. The globe
spins off its axis, smashes on the floor.

The telephone is ringing off the hook.
My daughter is all right.

For William and Teresa

Everything to be endured

you said, quoting Matthew Arnold,
and nothing to be done.
No fit theme for poetry. And I
remembered, sometime or other in school,
reading that. About *Empedocles*
on Etna—and then, I think, in Yeats,
who quoted it excluding Wilfred Owen from
his *Oxford Book of Modern Verse.*
You looked at me, hoping I would
understand, and yet I hadn't. . . . Because
you meant your *own* poems, those
you write and show to no one, those
that lie down darkly in some bottom drawer—
those, you thought, that did no more
than imitate a passive suffering.
I should have known.

But then what's passive
when a man of eighty-five, survivor
of two cancers, sits up all night long
to face his demons in the way he always has
and sees at dawn the black rectangle
on his desk he's made of darkness
hurled at eternity in words?
This is something to be done,
endured to be everything, fit theme
for any poem. Poems in the mind,
poems in the bottom drawer,
poems heading out past Jupiter like
mental probes launched at some far sun.
They're all the same.

You wouldn't choose
to write these poems but you are chosen.
That's endurance and the doing
and the fitness all in one. Where they go
and what becomes of them you'll never know.
If you kneel down before the winter hearth
to burn them, who's to say they'll not
be etched by fire on some unheard of stone
standing somewhere in an unknown city?

For Ernest Sandeen

In Praise of Fire

It has nobody else
except for the sun and me

*

It shows itself to the vagrant
it shows itself to the cunning
it shows itself to those in love

Nothing is lost in fire
but only condensed

*

At the edges of the fire
the objects which are not aglow
or otherwise remarkable
endure in someone else's time

The bird which alone makes the flock
flies out of the fire

Take a handful of ash
or of anything else that is past
and you will see that it is still on fire
or that it can be fire

Translated with Vladeta Vucković
from the Serbian of Branko Miljković

While You Are Singing

While you are singing
who will carry your burden?
While you alone defy
the poverty of clarity?

While you encounter bitter fruit
and the sarcastic dew
while you are singing
who will carry your burden?

Travel. Sing. Defy.
Only the poem desires you
and the night reveres you.
But while you are singing

Who will carry your burden?

Translated with Vladeta Vucković
from the Serbian of Branko Miljković

Private Poem

To a friend who made a Festival and notes a time & place,
defends the 'public sphere'

Fair and fair enough! So *not,* therefore,
in that Shelford sitting room alone,
10 September, 1973,
but on a bus, the upper deck,
somewhere between Trumpington & Cambridge
fully six months earlier
and in a goodly company of folk!
An idea's rare enough that if we're going
to credit the right person
we'd better also credit the right time & place?
Well, they've come and gone four times,
those homing birds, to and from
the singing school and slugging match,
and now, I think, you weary
of it all,
                demand the crystal clarities.

So it's like this—
              the black light that filters through
Seferis's *The Thrush,* through 1946,
through Ceri Richards' *Apple of Gower* & your poems
illuminates the private life alone
and not the 'public sphere'
however much we bellow out our lungs
in roaring, hybrid coliseums of fantasy. . . .
Clichés of theory!
Panels full of reborn, earnest suffragettes!
The black light's extinguished
in the white fluorescent light of meeting hall,
committee room, symposium and seminar.
Poems erased by Poetry.
Headlights on the routine, stupefying bus
burn into the crystal darkness
of a single room.

Public Poem

To the same, returning home from Belgrade
with his new book, 'The Manager'

We do not manage well! We do, however,
end our wanderings at some point
and come home. 1990
is as good a year as most;
and better, I suppose, counted out in pounds
than counted out in dinars.
But how fitting that the English now must
read your book on Thatcher's Britain
in Cyrillic! (You bring it home
with new wife and
new child.) Deciphering your codes,
grinning at your misdemeanors,
who prepared their case and sent you
into exile?

I take it back—
                    the white light that shines
from your new book, from 1989,
from wagers with the future that would wive
and father children
surely must illuminate the city & the street
however much we bitch in our bewilderment
and, alone in single rooms, disguise
the passing of our hour as black hermetic strength
and pull down all the blinds.
In Belgrade, Miljković once wrote: *While*
you are singing, who will carry
your burden? But while you carry
your burden, who will sing your song?
Those deciphering your codes,
grinning at your misdemeanors, those
who made their case & sent you
into exile.

Footnote on a Gift
for Laura

My friend, your teacher, gives you Rilke's *Elegies,*
reminding you that Rilke lived in Prague
when he was young. You are off to Prague
and you are young, but not as young as Rilke was
when he abandoned what he later called
a city of subordinate existences where, perhaps,
the danger was you might wake up one sunny morning
to discover you had turned into a cockroach.
But you, Laura, are already learning Czech
and do not fear in Deutsch to find subordinate
the things of new Bohemia. May everybody thrive there!
And may you thrive there with them,
teaching English which, I hope, will help them read
computer manuals & scientific articles but not,
like German once, create a separate class of citizens.
If you are not as visionary as Rainer Maria
then you are, at least, more sane. The last thing
in this world I could imagine is that you,
with all your sensible charm, would ever want
to hug an Angel rather than a human being.
You're also saner than your crazy father
who has had a dreadful year, and whose scribblings
these days sputter & meander foolishly.
He'd better, therefore, keep this short
and just say that he'll miss you.
And if you do see Angels hover over Prague,
stand still and wait. They'll fly away.
You need not whisper to the city or yourself
a misconceived intransitive—*subordinate.*

Two Poems

I—The Egyptian

Where you descend, depth exists no more.
It was enough that I took your breath away in a reed
For a seed to burst in the desert under my heel.

It all came at a single blow, and nothing remains.
Nothing but the mark on my door
Made by the embalmer's burning hands.

II—The Urn

Endlessly to watch a second night come on
While looking through this sluggish lucid pyre
Which doesn't even yield any ash!

But the mouth at the end, the mouth that's full
Of earth and rage,
Remembers that it is itself which burns

And guides the cradles on the river.

Translated from the French of Jacques Dupin

Fragments After Hamsun

I

And you who sit up
in the darkness of your cell
and see a glowing word
before your eyes: KUBOAA.

Who's to tell you that
your word must signify *tobacco shop?*
Who will say KUBOAA
must mean *cattle show* or *queen?*

Who's insisting on *heraldic bird*
or *sunrise?* Who will threaten
you with words like *bread* and *key?*

II

The man who hungers now, who thirsts,
is made of words like *abattoir*
himself, although he thinks he's made
of *sunrise, bread* and *key.*

KUBOAA seeks Amanuensis for
his creature with a pen
whose lips still murmur FUHRER
north of Bergen!

Free Translation and Recombination: Fragments from Octavio Paz

"No ví girar las formas hasta desvanecerse
En claridad inmóvil . . ."

*

By negation is my increase, my wealth.
Lord, Lord of erosions and dispersions,
I come to you in the whirlwind.

Into the oldest tree I drive my nail.

*

In the architecture of silence
Is no debate between the bees
And the statistics.

Nor is there any dialectic among apes.

The wind blows. The rain obliterates
The mason's mark. On every psalm (on every
Mask of lime) a crown of fire appears.

*

To rattle semantic seeds:
To bury the word, the kernel of fire,
In the body of Ceres:

poem, poem

Spilling the water and wine,
Spilling the fire.

*

Shake the book like a branch,
Detaching a phrase:

Voices and laughter,
Dancing and tambourines.

This is the winter solstice,
Who will awaken the stones?

Shake the book, detaching a word:
Pollywog, poison, periwig . . .

Say it: a penance of words.

*

But the huddled men in the alleys,
The huddled men in the squares & the mosques,
They took my gems and my grave-clothes.

    I was covered with poems.

In the center of incandescence,
In the column of noon,
I was ringed with sand and insomnia.

    I was covered with poems.

*

And the sophistry of clocks.
And the provinces of abstract towns.

Dizzy geometries, vertigoes.

Not to foretell but to tell.
To say it: a paring away.

Nombre Antiguo del Fuego

    in the tunnels of onyx
      the circles of salt,
   chimerical child of
     calculus and of thirst:

From every stone appears a brief black tongue
Naming the scales of the night.

Horace Augustus Mandelstam Stalin

A poem for The Leader, either way,
but Horace found it easier.
The widow of the Russian heard for weeks
an *Os* an *Os* an *Os*—
repeating syllable of Stalin's Ode
metamorphosed as a wasp
in the iron air of Voronezh.

Imagine Mandelstam a gentle and
official poet patronized by a patrician
like Maecenas and a friend of Caesar's.
"Octavian," he'd say.
Or: "Joseph Vissarionovich."
The syllables that trail along the poems
begotten by the Stalin Ode he tried
to write say *Os*
Os, Os . . .

      wasp, axle, exile.

Others found it easier.
When their tongues were cut out, wrote
Nadezhda in her book, *still*
they praised him with their wagging stubs.

Into Cyrillic

I see they've written ПРИЈАТЕЉСТВО,
but it's Greek to me. They sign
it with my name. Something's been
translated, something here is very strange.

They've written ЦОН and METAJAC
and they say it isn't Greek, they say
it isn't Russian either and I see
my name. I point to Macedonia,

to Leningrad. But everything, they
tell me, points to Kosovo. Everything
they tell me points to Sarajevo too.
For example, ПРИЈАТЕЉСТВО.

I ask them, did I write that word?
They found it in my poem. They say I stood
with Miloš Obilić in 1389: everybody
heard me shouting LAZARUS!

I tell them I was silent; if there, I stood
aside. They say I stood among
the Yugovići as in 1989 I stood between
Milosović and Karadžić.

I'm tangled in Cyrillic and I cannot
find my way. They'll help me.
They'll lead me on. I say I want to be
led out of this, away.

They say ПРИЈАТЕЉСТВО!
The trains have all stopped running and
there is no petrol for the cars.
Everyone is shouting ЦОН, ЦОН, ЦОН!

Bogomil in Languedoc

One stone at Domazan is enough.
In southern France among
the Catharist sarcophagi beyond
a village full of tiled roofs.

He is the warrior of Radimlja and he
has come this far. He raises both his arms.
He spreads wide both enormous hands.
Although he is entirely silent here,

his mason, up from Tuscany and
proselytizing slogs along the hot Apennine,
spouted bits he'd learned from
Interrogatio Johannis to his missionary

friend who left the book at Carcassonne.
When all matter is to be destroyed,
the stone warrior here at Domazan
will give the sign. He will finally

drop his arms. And where he stood
the hole in space will spread until
all nothing speaks in tongues to no one.
May he, then, forever raise his hands.

The Singer of Tales
for Charles Simic

I

It's a strange sound
the first time you hear it

it's a kind of moan
& the old man bows in his lap

on the one taut string
of his *gusle*

warming up as if he were a kind of
West Virginian or a

Smoky Mountain fiddler
but the blues he has to play

the sorrow he will tell goes back
six hundred years

then it was almost too much to bear
but now he sings

II

Nothing of it written down
before the 1600s

They fled from Maritsa from Kosovo
the final loss at Smederevo

and settled where they could
around Regusa in the islands

146

on the Adriatic coast or Herzegovina
in Bosnia the Montenegrin hills

No one saw quite what had happened yet
No one sang about it

III

Then somebody did
Sang until his song recalled

the blackbirds from the field the bones
from shallow graves the banners

from oblivion the ichor bleeding from
the wounded ikon in the monastery's corner room

Sang until his voice failed utterly to sing
and then he moaned

and then he whispered weeping
in the whispering dark air

Now it is almost too much to bear
but then he sang

The Silence of Stones

I

In Bosnia, in Herzegovina nearby: enigmatic
standing stones proclaim
some mode of life that lost its way

upon the very field of light
where men and women danced the *kolo* once
and called to vine and lily,

wheeling sun and sickle moon, sheep and deer
and falcon: brother, sister.
Where the waters of Radimlja dry in dusty summer

enormous hands on the sarcophagi
spread their fingers wide in greeting or in admonition.
Hieratic, fetishistic.

Long before Lord Tvrtko left for Kosovo.

II

Some mode of life. Some field of light.
Before the list of Manichaean crimes
Drawn up by Torquemada for the Pope in Rome,

The Pope in Avignon was heard to whisper
Dobri Bosniani to his agents
up from Languedoc, reminding them of speech that

crawleth like a crab & heretics who *creepeth in humility*
upon St. Catherine's Eve when conflagration
would consume the hills and plains, the rocks and trees,

falcons, sheep, and wild deer
of that far place already near brought down before
Lord Tvrtko left for Kosovo

Where raised hands admonish or salute.

III

Admonish or salute. Some mode of life,
some field of light whereon they dance the *kolo*
holding hands, where feet tread gently

in the dust beside the dry and stony bed of the Radimlja.
On stećak, mramor, upright slab or obelisk,
40,000 hands rise up in solemn gesture of some last

refusal or compliance, join together then
beneath the wheeling sun, the sickle moon, there among
the animals and calligraphic ornament,

vine & lily, brother falcon, sister lamb or fawn,
Dobri Bosniani spoken for
in Avignon but silent on this silent plain

Long before and after Tvrtko left for Kosovo.

After Years Away

I — My Bed, My Father's Bell

First my bed, then his, now mine again—
just for a week.

He died in it, my father, where for years
I'd lie beside my pretty love,

alive and indiscreet.
He moved in here so she, my mother,

might sleep undisturbed while he gazed darkly
all night long into the dark.

In need, he'd ring a small brass bell
molded in the shape

of a hoop-skirted lady
sweeping with a broom and looking grim.

I see it now,
lying sideways on a row of books.

He'd ring it and she'd come to him.

II — My Father's Bell, My Grandfather's Books

The books are remnants of a city gardener's
life: the works of Emerson,

a Tennyson collected, *Paradise Lost*.
He's written in his Milton

1650
1608

42 years. And on the title page:
Begun in January, 1893, and never finished.

In another hand: *Happy new year to you, 1892.*
He's figured that J.M. was 42 in 1650

when he wrote his answer to Salmasius
and lost his sight.

Defensio pro Populo Anglicano.
At the Presbyterian funeral a cousin

asked: *are you religious?* and I said
in callow family disaffection:

Gnostic. Bogomil. Albigensian for heaven's sake.
On the *Ex Libris* plate:

Poetry. This book will not be loaned.
And underneath: *couldn't dig this month.*

Ground as cold as hell.
I replace the book. I pick up the bell.

III — My Mother's Broom, My Father's Bell

My mother stashed those books in here
for me to find. My father

would have seen them, reaching for his bell,
but they were not for him.

She left them here, her father's only legacy,
as she began to sweep.

She swept the hearth, the porch and drive,
she even swept the street.

(She swept my father once entirely
off his feet.)

While he lay dying & while I sat reading books,
she swept his mortal breath away,

I think.
When she heard the ringing here . . .

And then swept circles round & round the bier
as I said *Gnostic, Bogomil.*

Although the ground was cold as hell
they dug the grave & dug it deep.

Sweet sleep. Sweep sweep.
There's no one here to listen or to care,

and so I ring the bell—
creating great commotion *there.*

Dedication to a Cycle of Poems on the Pilgrim Routes to Santiago de Compostela

This is for my daughter, who,
in the middle of the map I try to draw, the making,
struggles to a Compostela of her own

in pain & torment. *What did I do wrong?* she asks.
What did I do wrong
to suffer this?—The primal, secret, terrified & universal

query of the sick. She did nothing wrong.
And yet she walks in chains
along a Lemosina or a Tolosona Dolorosa

winding through uncertainty & grief
to disappear into unknowable remote far distances.
She walks ahead of me, doubting that

I follow, although I call out loudly & I try.
But also, when she herself must rest, unable to go on,
at hospital or hospice on the way, then

I'll learn to wait, a patient too, without impatience.
Perhaps we'll see pass by every single other living soul!
The routes were arduous, each one,

and cemeteries in the churchyards far outnumber
monuments recording cures miraculous
achieved along the way. You had to get there somehow.

You had to show the saint your poor
tormented frail human body. You had to drag it there
driven by your guilt or your desire.

The journey's so entirely strange I cannot fathom it.
And yet this map, this prayer:
That she will somehow get to Compostela,

take that how you may, & that I will be allowed to follow.
And that Santiago, call him what you like,
Son of Thunder, Good Saint Jacques, The Fisherman,

Or whoever really lies there—
hermit, heretic, shaman healer with no name—
will somehow make us whole.

Notes and Sources

Part I: Tags from Yeats, Joyce, de Sade, Octavio Paz, Marianne Moore, and Jean Cocteau ("For John, After His Visit"). **Part II:** F. S. Howes, *The English Musical Renaissance* ("Once for English Music"). Edmund Wilson, *To the Finland Station* ("Three Around a Revolution" and "Bakunin in Italy"). Ezra Pound, "Cino" ("E. P. In Crawfordsville"). Kurt Seligmann, *A History of Magic* ("Six for Michael Anania"). Paul Hindemith, *Libretto: Matis der Maler;* Otto Benesch, *The Art of the Renaissance in Northern Europe,* chapter II; Ian Kemp, *Hindemith;* F. W. Sternfeld, ed., *Music in the Modern Age,* chapter 2: "Germany", Elaine Padmore; Norman Cohn, *The Pursuit of the Millennium* ("Double Sonnet on the Absence of Text: 'Symphony Matis der Maler', Berlin, 1934:—Metamorphoses"). Julian Tennyson, *Suffolk Scene* ("Brandon, Breckland: The Flint Knappers"). Julian of Norwich, *Revelations of Divine Love* (in the Clifton Wolters translation); P. Franklin Chambers, *Juliana of Norwich: an Introductory Appreciation and an Interpretive Anthology* ("59 Lines Assembled Quickly Sitting on a Wall Near the Reconstruction of the Lady Juliana's Cell"). R. A. Edwards, *The Fighting Bishop:* R. B. Dobson, ed., *The Peasants' Revolt of 1381;* Rodney Hilton, *Bond Men Made Free;* Norman Cohn, *The Pursuit of the Millennium* ("26 June 1381/1977"). Thomas Hardy, *Jude the Obscure;* H. T. Lowe Porter, translator's note, *Dr. Faustus;* A. F. E. Burroughs, *West Midland Dialects of the Fourteenth Century;* J. Matthias, *Bucyrus* and "Th' Entencioun and Speche of Philosophres"; tags from King Alfred, Chaucer, Langland, John of Mandeville, Wycliffe, the *Pearl* poet, Joseph of Arimathaea; George Steiner, *Language and Silence* ("Turns"). **Part III:** R. B. Dobson, ed., *The Peasants' Revolt of 1381* ("Spokesman to Bailiff, 1349: Plague"). C. J. Stranks, *St. Etheldreda: Queen and Abbess; The Book of Margery Kempe* in the W. Butler-Bowdon translation ("Two Ladies"). Sir Geoffrey Keynes, ed., *Sir Thomas Browne: Selected Writings* ("Words for Sir Thomas Browne"). Justin Kaplan, *Mr. Clemens and Mark Twain;* Mark Twain, "The Celebrated Jumping Frog of Calavaras County" ("Mark Twain in the Fens"). Joanna Richardson, *Verlaine;* Enid Starkie, *Arthur Rimbaud;* Paul Verlaine, *Sagesse* ("Paul Verlaine in Lincolnshire"). César Vallejo, "Agape" from *Los Heraldos Negros* ("Agape"). *The Great Tournament Roll of Westminster, A Collotype Reproduction of the Manuscript:* Sidney Anglo's Historical Introduction, Appendices I and II—Tiptoft's Ordinances and the Revels Account of Richard Gibson, and the Analytical Description; Gordon Donaldson, *Scottish Kings;* Lt. Colonel Howard Green, *Battlefields of Britain and Ireland;* Peter Alexander, Introduction to Shakespeare's (?) *Henry VIII* in the Collins Tudor Shakespeare ("Double Derivation, Association, & Cliché: from *The Great Tournament Roll of Westminster*"). Thomas Nashe, "A Litany in Time of Plague" ("Clarifications for Robert Jacoby"). Johan Huizinga, *Homo Ludens; The Manual of Horsemanship of the British Horse Society and Pony Club;* Lars Norén, "August"; tags from John Berryman, W. B. Yeats, Robert Hass, Wordsworth, *King Lear*

("Poem for Cynouai"). **Part IV:** Tacitus, *The Annals of Imperial Rome,* chapters 10 and 11; Stephen Gosson, *School of Abuse;* R. R. Clarke, *East Anglia,* chapters 6 and 7; I. A. Richmond, *Roman Britain,* Chapters 1, 2, and 5; Donald R. Dudley and Graham Webster, *The Rebellion of Boudicca;* Patrick Crampton, *Stonehenge of the Kings,* chapter 1 ("East Anglian Poem"). Joseph Swetnam, "Epistle to the Reader" and "Preface to Professors" in *The Noble Science of Defence;* George Silver, *The Paradoxes of Defence* and *Brief Instructions Upon My Paradoxes of Defence;* J. D. Aylward, *The English Masters of Arms;* A.L.Soens, "Lawyers, Collusions and Cudgels: Middleton's *Anything For a Quiet Life,* I.i. 220-21", *English Language Notes,* Vol. VII, No. 4 ("The Noble Art of Fence: A Letter"). "Cambridge Spinning-House: Rules and Regulations," 21 February 1854 ("A Cambridge Spinning-House: Henry John Temple Palmerston's Syllabics for Marianne Moore"). Sir John Rothenstein, *Modern British Painters,* Vols. 1, 2, and 3 ("Mr. Rothenstein's Rudiments"). W. G. Arnott, *Orwell Estuary;* George Ewart Evans, *Ask the Fellows Who Cut the Hay;* Julia Pipe, *Port on the Alde;* Rudyard Kipling, "A Smuggler's Song"; Richard Cobbold, *The History of Margaret Catchpole* ("Lines for the Gentlemen" and "More Lines for the Gentlemen"). Abel Gance, *Napoleon* ("At a Screening of Gance's *Napoleon:* Arts Theatre, Cambridge"). François Villon, "L'Epitaphe Villon"; Mrs. Thatcher on The Falklands, quoted in *Le Monde;* Neil Lands, *The French Pyrenees;* E. Cortade, *Collioure: Guide Historique et Touristique;* Yves Bonnefoy, "Jean et Jeanne"; Antonio Machado, "El sol es un globo de fuego"; Guiraud Riquièr, "Be'm degra de chantar tener . . ."; Stéphane Mallarmé, "Prose—pour des Esseintes" ("A Wind in Roussillon"). **Part V:** *Grimm's Fairy Tales,* trans. Margaret Hunt with an introduction by Frances Clarke Sayers ("Not Having Heard a Single Fairy Tale"). Branko Miljković, "Pohvala Vatri" ("In Praise of Fire"). Branko Miljković, "Dok Budeš Pevao" ("While You Are Singing"); Jacques Dupin, "L'Égyptienne" and "L'Urne" ("Two Poems"). Knute Hamsun, *Hunger* ("Fragments After Hamsun"). Octavio Paz, "Salamandra" and "Ladera Este" ("Free Translation and Recombination: Fragments from Octavio Paz"); Osip Mandelstam, "Lines on Stalin"; Nadezhda Mandelstam, *Hope Against Hope* ("Horace Augustus Mandelstam Stalin"); "Friendship," reprinted in the present book, as translated into Serbian by Ivan Lalic; the Serbian word in the first line is the title of the poem; the other Serbian words are my Christian name and surname ("Into Cyrillic"). Oto Bihalji-Merin and Alojz Benac, *Bogomil Sculpture;* Jacques Lacarriere, *The Gnostics* ("Bogomil in Languedoc" and "The Silence of Stones"). Svetozar Koljević, *The Epic In The Making;* Albert B. Lord, *The Singer of Tales;* Rebecca West, *Black Lamb and Grey Falcon* ("The Singer of Tales").

I should note that the "Dedication to a Cycle of Poems on the Pilgrim Routes to Santiago de Compostela" which concludes this book was originally intended to initiate "A Compostela Diptych," the third and longest poem in my volume called *A Gathering of Ways.* For a number of reasons it was not, finally, printed in that context. Nonetheless, I would like to acknowledge the original intention.

A Note about the Author

A native of Ohio, John Matthias teaches English at the University of Notre Dame. He has been Visiting Fellow in Poetry at Clare Hall, Cambridge, and lived for much of the 1970s in the East Anglia region of England. He has published four previous volumes of poetry with Swallow Press: *Bucyrus* (1971), *Turns* (1975), *Crossing* (1979), and *Northern Summer: New and Selected Poems* (1984). *Bathory & Lermontov* (1980) and *Två Dikter* (1989) were published in Sweden. With Göran Printz-Påhlson, he edited and translated *Contemporary Swedish Poetry* (Swallow, 1980) and with Vladeta Vučković he translated *The Battle of Kosovo* (Swallow, 1987). His own work has been translated into Swedish, Dutch, French, German, Greek, and Serbo-Croat. He has edited *23 Modern British Poets* (Swallow, 1971), *Introducing David Jones* (Faber and Faber, 1980), and *David Jones: Man and Poet* (The National Poetry Foundation, 1989). Simultaneously with this book, Swallow Press is publishing *Beltane at Aphelion: Longer Poems*.